B. F. (Benjamin Franklin) Scribner

How Soldiers were made

Or, The War as I saw it

B. F. (Benjamin Franklin) Scribner

How Soldiers were made
Or, The War as I saw it

ISBN/EAN: 9783337133580

Printed in Europe, USA, Canada, Australia, Japan

Cover: Foto ©ninafisch / pixelio.de

More available books at **www.hansebooks.com**

HOW SOLDIERS WERE MADE;

OR

THE WAR AS I SAW IT

UNDER

BUELL, ROSECRANS, THOMAS, GRANT AND SHERMAN.

BY

B. F. SCRIBNER,

LATE COLONEL THIRTY-EIGHTH INDIANA VETERAN VOLUNTEERS, AND BREVET BRIGA-
DIER-GENERAL, COMMANDING BRIGADE, FIRST DIVISION, FOURTEENTH
ARMY CORPS, ARMY OF THE CUMBERLAND.

NEW ALBANY, IND.
1887.

COPYRIGHT,
1887.
BY B. F. SCRIBNER.

Donohue & Henneberry, Printers and Binders, Chicago.

DEDICATION.

To My Comrades in the War for the Union this Book is Inscribed, with Reverence for the Dead and Greetings to the Living.

PREFACE.

THE subjects herein treated have been so well portrayed by skillful writers, and so thoroughly described by officers of high rank, with all the help of statistical information, and with complete official reports at hand, that to enter the field without such equipment would seem egotistical and superfluous. I deem it proper, therefore, to explain the motives which prompt me to this undertaking.

The works of Generals Grant, Thomas and Sherman, together with the official documents issued from the War Department, afford all that could be desired to make history, and yet leave ample room for works of less pretension. My purpose is to describe the events as they appeared to me from the position of my rank, command and location. Not having been in possession of the plans and intentions of my chief, I will not attempt the official exactness so well accomplished in the works above referred to, but will deal with such experiences as soldiers talk about when they meet each other at their re-unions and camp-fires. It is also my desire to treat the subject in an introspective manner, from a personal standpoint; from the inner life; emotionally and subjectively, and thereby refresh in the minds of my comrades their own impressions and feelings.

In mitigation of the charge of vanity displayed by this course, reference is made to the fact that a story related by an eye-witness, even if unskillfully told, possesses a certain interest, and that those most capable of describing stirring and tragic events may not happen to be at hand to be moved and inspired by them.

CONTENTS.

CHAPTER I.

The clouds gather and break — Southern sympathy — A divided community — My service in the Mexican War — The Spencer Grays offer their services — The Battle of Buena Vista — Fort Sumter fired upon — The shock and agony thereat — The Union sentiment aroused — Gov. Morton organizes the Indiana Legion — My appointment as colonel in it — The making of soldiers commenced — Inward struggles — Gov. Morton consulted — Waiting for my turn — The Twenty-third go to the field — A borrowed sword — More inward struggles — Duty prevails — Appointed colonel Thirty-eighth Indiana Volunteers. 11

CHAPTER II.

Gen. Robert Anderson in command at Louisville — Buckner's threatened invasion — The Thirty-eighth joins Sherman at Lebanon Junction — Wade Rolling Fork, march upon Elizabethtown, Ky., and drive out rebel cavalry there — We take position at Muldraugh Hill — Short rations and incomplete equipments — The long roll — To arms — A false alarm — A council of war in which no counsel was asked — Another interview with Gen. Sherman in which I do the talking — Traits of Sherman — The column advances to Bacon Creek — We enter upon the business of making soldiers — The typhoid fever obstructs — We move on to Green River — Willick's Thirty-second Indiana has a fight — A Texas regiment under Col. Terry defeated — Col. Terry killed — Whipped by the Dutch

— More sickness — A hard winter — We march and countermarch — On to Bowling Green — Buckner evacuates — We make our entry into Nashville — I am ordered on a board of commissioners — Schemes to defraud the government — We are transferred from McCook's Division to that of O. M. Mitchell — We try to catch cavalry with infantry — A fifty-one mile march in one day — Rebel Gen. Adams driven across the Tennessee — Another expedition — We cross the Cumberland Mountains — Skirmish at Sweeden's Cove — Chattanooga threatened — A perilous recrossing of the mountains at night — A hard march to Tullahoma — Only a mile to camp — On the march again — The army assembles at Battle Creek — Rousseau supersedes Mitchell — I write a letter to Rousseau — The Thirty-eighth assigned to Ninth Brigade under Gen. Sill — We are sent to Deckard — Buell and Bragg on a race to Louisville — Buell comes out ahead — Battle of Perryville — The pursuit of Bragg...... 20

CHAPTER III.

I am assigned to the command of the Brigade — Gen. Rosecrans relieves Buell — Edgefield Junction — Rebel stores captured at Springfield, Tenn. — A new flag presented to the Thirty-eighth at Camp Andy Johnson — Battle of Stone River 64

CHAPTER IV.

Bad weather — Railroad destroyed by guerrillas — Short forage — How to convoy a train — Working out war problems — Foraging expeditions — A predicament — A pleasure party spoiled — That's shucks — A hard road to travel — A change for the better — Comfortable quarters — Our wives and lady friends from home visit us — Guerrillas attack the train — Why don't he stop the firing? — Gay times — Anecdote of Libby Prison — All Fools' day — Gen. Thomas gives a lesson in drawing — Brigade drills — An expedition toward Hoover's Gap — The missing sentinel — Bugle calls and signals 87

CHAPTER V.

The Tullahoma campaign — The country overflowed by rain — A sharp combat at Hoover's Gap — Uninvited guests to dinner — Anderson's Station — More good times — Vallandigham visits the South — His advice to his friends — The logic of events modifies opinions — The Southern women — Their beauty, intelligence and prejudices — The hardships of Southern Union men — Lincolnian philosophy — Horrors of war — War not all evil. 121

CHAPTER VI.

Our hotel at Anderson — More mountain climbing — Dug Gap — We escape from a trap — Hay fever again — The Battle of Chickamauga — A metaphorical hurricane — A night of gloom — Followed by a day of glory — We bring off the rear — Gen. Thomas in bivouac — A characteristic interview with him — Position at Rossville — We again bring off the rear.................... 139

CHAPTER VII.

A great battle; its length, breadth and thickness — Bragg's efforts to cut off our supplies — He succeeds in shortening our rations — Gen. Thomas relieves Rosecrans — Grant and Sherman join us — Grant in command — The army reorganized — The Battle of Lookout Mountain — "Not scared but exhausted" — The men assume command and charge up Mission Ridge — The emotion of victory — Pursuit of Bragg — Adventures of a night — A South Carolina major — A sleepy town — At Taylor's Ridge we fight by the book — Headquarters on Cameron Hill — A freak of nature.............165

CHAPTER VIII.

Incidents before and after the battle — Crossing the Tennessee on pontoons — The horse boat at Brown's Ferry — The negro philosopher at Ringgold — The astronomical Joe — Pete's appeal — Mr. Anderson again — He wants his Mary — An interview with Lieut. Col. Griffin — More inward struggles — The Thirty-eighth re-enlist as veterans — Influence of a few over many — Different kinds of good officers — How field officers are estranged by tattlers and mischief-makers — Lieut. Col. Griffin, his lovable character — The Thirty-eighth on veteran furlough. 196

CHAPTER IX.

The Atlanta campaign — A hint to critics — Arms and ammunition tested — Buzzard Roost and Rocky Face — A grand and heroic advance — Sharpshooters — How two can play at the same game — A peace conquered — Barney's fears of goblins — The toothless recruit — The Battle of Resaca...................220

CHAPTER X.

The capture of Rome — Pursuit of Johnston — McPherson in trouble at Dallas — Seeking the rebels' right — The night battle at New Hope Church — We are complimented in orders — The cracker line again established — Johnston yields Allatoona Pass — The evolution of the soldier — Fighting Joe Hooker — State prejudices overcome — Regulars and volunteers in harmony — Learning how to behave — The soldiers' settlement of the knapsack question — Sherman's liberal allowance of baggage to officers — Wash day interrupted — Old tactics criticised — Old and new troops contrasted — How breastworks were made — Hardships increased by the rain — Trenches and rifle-pits overflowed — A rebel's opinion that bullets are impartial — A lady's wardrobe sought at brigade headquarters — The chagrin at finding it.... 237

CHAPTER XI.

More rain — A battle in a thunder-storm — Leather Breeches a hero — We relieve Gen. Harker at Kenesaw — Are furiously bombarded — The lines still advance — We relieve Gen. Kimball at Bald Knob — The soldier still develops — The safest place in battle — The best strategy — How to win victory — How an officer gains the respect of his men — How he loses it — Rousseau's popularity with the men accounted for — An analysis of his character — Some advice to the future volunteer — Joe Redding — Incidents of his career 266

CHAPTER XII.

More about Bald Knob — The soldier as a wit — Illustrative anecdotes — The dog story — A soldier's reasons for a furlough — A circus rider's feats — The various trades of the men and their utility — Leather Breeches again — His contract is violated — He is deceived thereby — A substitute for a battery — Artillery-men's prejudice against bullets from small arms — Leather Breeches is scarce of horses — Sherman exposes himself to danger — He is expostulated with — Interview with Gen. Thomas — Incidents connected with him — The assault of Kenesaw — Frightful loss — Sherman decides to abandon his communications and to turn the rebel flank — Our division delegated to hold the left and to fortify it — We work all night — The enemy gone next morning — A close pursuit — Atlanta approached — I break down — Am sent to the rear — My mortification thereat — Hallucinations — A shirk's excuse — I am sent home — My hay fever approaches — My resignation — Our country's generosity to her soldiers — What she cannot pay for 284

CONCLUSION 308

CHAPTER I.

THE CLOUDS GATHER AND BREAK.

NEW ALBANY, Ind., my birthplace and home, is situated on the Ohio river opposite the large and flourishing city of Louisville, Ky. The social and business relations between the two cities have always been intimate. The Louisville daily papers are simultaneously delivered by carriers to subscribers in both cities. New Albany, before the war, was extensively engaged in the building of steamboats. The largest and fleetest boats which plied the Ohio, Mississippi and other rivers in the South were built here. These and other considerations tended to make New Albany essentially a southern city, and to cause her to share with the South the same principles and prejudices. Therefore at the beginning of the secession movement after the election of Mr. Lincoln, the public sentiment of the majority sympathized with the South, and was opposed to the idea of coercion. Public assemblies were nightly held, and the questions involved were discussed with heated acrimony. At these meetings it was frequently asserted that "if coercion was attempted by the North it should be over the dead body of the speaker." Others declared that "if the South was forced to separate, the dividing line should be drawn north of New Albany." Reproaches, accusations and denunciations prevailed; families were divided, and the ties of friendship severed. There was, however, amid all this strife and division, a minority who were for the Union without an "if," and who were hopeful that blows and bloodshed would be avoided.

I had been a soldier during the Mexican War, and became twenty-one years of age before my time of enlistment expired. I took part in the hard-fought and bloody battle of Buena Vista, where Gen. Taylor with 4,500 men withstood Santa Anna with 22,000. After the war was over, I published a little book containing extracts from my private journal entitled "Camp Life of a Volunteer, by One Who Saw the Elephant."

The Spencer Grays, the name of the company to which I belonged, was, previous to the war, one of the uniformed companies of the city and had acquired quite a local reputation for soldierly qualities. We had taken the first prize at a military encampment held at Louisville; this stimulated us to greater proficiency and ripened us for the war when it came. The news of Gen. Taylor's victories at Palo Alto and Resaca De La Palma and his subsequent reported danger there fanned us into a blaze of enthusiasm. We offered our services to Gov. Whitcomb to help Gen. Taylor, and were accepted as soon as the call for troops was issued. We were mustered in for a year as a company, under our old organization, and were assigned to the Second Regiment Indiana Volunteers, commanded by Col. William A. Bowles, who to the incapacity displayed in this position, added disloyalty and treachery during the war for the Union.

I had thus at the breaking out of the rebellion some experience, and my taste for military tactics thus early acquired has clung to me to this day. I was now animated with patriotism; the flag of the Union was to me a sacred object, and I could not bring myself to believe that the American people would insult or assail it. Therefore, when Fort Sumpter was fired upon, I was overcome with surprise, awe and grief; I felt all the horrors of impending war and, with almost prophetic intuitions, comprehended its magnitude and the sacrifices that would be involved in it. By the firing upon Fort Sumpter the overt act was committed which did much to strengthen and unite the friends of the Union. A military enthusiasm was awakened; companies were formed and the streets echoed with the shrill notes of the fife and the roll and the rattle of the drum; the spirit of war filled the air and permeated the minds of all, and the Union sentiment became dominant and aggressive. Soldiers for the Confederate army, openly recruited in Louisville, no longer exhibited themselves from the decks of steamboats which touched at our wharves on their way South, and boats from the South no longer flaunted from their flag-staffs rebellious emblems.

Gov. Morton, as best he could under the militia laws of the State, proceeded to organize the Indiana Legion, and I was appointed colonel of the seventh regiment, third brigade, and the task of forming companies and establishing drills and parades was at once undertaken. The change of tactics from Scott to Hardee made· it necessary to learn them all over again, which involved much study and practice. In the meantime the 75,000 men called for had gone to the front, and the enlistment to fill the quota of Indiana for a call just made for three hundred thousand more, had commenced. Some ·two thousand men were soon enrolled in the legion; officers and men vied with each other in diligence to acquire the duties of the soldier; night after night at the various rendezvous throughout the city could be heard inspiring martial music and the commands of the drill; the people were earnest, active and determined that the Union should be preserved.

A new trouble now assailed me; what should be done with these men, many of whom were ready to enlist for the war? Already they had been overheard talking among themselves, showing a willingness to go, and the ever-recurring question would overwhelm me. Whose duty is it to lead in this matter? The question could not be evaded, but continually confronted me, imperiously demanding an answer. The anxiety of mind occasioned by contending struggles between my sense of duty and inclinations, and my personal interests and family ties, gave me great distress at the time, and even now I shrink from its contemplation. At length the conclusion was reached to advise with Gov. Morton upon the subject, and a visit to Indianapolis for that purpose was made. I represented to the governor that a regiment of men could be enlisted from my command. My humiliation was manifested that expressions of willingness to serve their country in this emergency should first come from sources other than the commanding officer. It was tauntingly charged that the cause and responsibility of the war rested upon the party to which we belonged. But I had a large and increasing family to provide for and an extensive and complicated business to manage, and the position of colonel in a regiment, which would be an improvement in the condition of many men, to me would be financial ruin. I assured him that I would place myself in his hands whenever he thought it was my turn to take up arms again, or that it was the duty of one situated as I was to offer his services, and I would solemnly promise to do as he should decide, and to serve at any time in any capacity in which he should call me. The governor treated me with much kindness and consideration and greatly relieved my mind by his assurances that he would not fail to call upon me when he thought it was my turn. He urged me to continue my efforts to develop military enthusiasm, and to encourage enlistment to fill the quota for Indiana.

The Twenty-third Indiana Regiment was organized, and William L. Sanderson, my captain during the Mexican War, was appointed its colonel, and when the regiment was ready for the field it was escorted to the station by the legion with our cheers and blessings.

My internal struggles with contending convictions of duty now returned with augmented force and disturbed my sleep and made me restless and wretched. I had made some reputation at the battle of Buena Vista, and had been praised and embraced on the field by our brigade-commander, Gen. Joseph Lane, afterward senator from Oregon and candidate for Vice-President on the ticket with Breckinridge. The citizens of New Albany had presented me with a handsome sword of honor. In my reply to the presentation address, I intimated that it was accepted as a loan, and that should my country ever need a sword for its defense, my arm should go with it. Some talk about this borrowed sword greatly disturbed me. Every mail brought me offers of detachments and companies, and I felt like one who would do nothing himself, yet would stand in the way of others. Goaded on by these painful emotions, at length my mind was made up. My difficulties had been augmented by the precarious health of my wife, which made it important that she should be kept quiet and free from worry or excitement; but the birth of a daughter somewhat relieved me of this source of anxiety. I was now ready to act, and without further delay or advice I hurried to the telegraph office and sent the following dispatch:

"NEW ALBANY, IND., Aug. 21, 1861.
To Gov. O. P. Morton or the Secretary of War, Washington, D. C.:
I have a regiment of men nearly ready for service; do you want them?"

There was no call for troops, the requisition for three hundred thousand having been filled, yet within an hour the purport of the following reply was received from Gov. Morton, who was then in Washington:

"You are accepted. Report to Adjutant-General Noble at Indianapolis."
   (Signed)   O. P. MORTON.

Thus the die was cast, the Rubicon crossed, and within thirty days from the date of these dispatches I was in the field at the head of the Thirty-Eighth Indiana Volunteers.

CHAPTER II.

WE ARE OFF TO THE WARS AND THE FIGHT BEGINS.

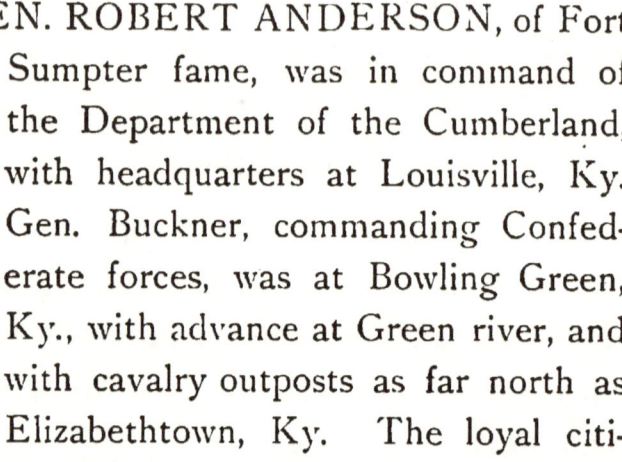GEN. ROBERT ANDERSON, of Fort Sumpter fame, was in command of the Department of the Cumberland, with headquarters at Louisville, Ky. Gen. Buckner, commanding Confederate forces, was at Bowling Green, Ky., with advance at Green river, and with cavalry outposts as far north as Elizabethtown, Ky. The loyal citizens of Louisville were in alarm from apprehension of an attack which all the circumstances tended to confirm; almost daily, committees and delegations of representative Union men visited my camp to urge upon me the necessity of being ready to assist them at a moment's notice. The Thirty-Eighth was mustered in on the 18th of September, 1861, by Capt. Gilman, U. S. A., and on the same day Gen. Anderson summoned me for consultation. He represented to me that

Buckner was daily expected; that at any hour the news of his approach might be received, that he had no adequate force to resist him, and he needed my services. A telegram was at once sent to Gov. Morton for his consent, and his reply was favorable, provided Gen. Anderson would equip me. The demand upon the government to provide arms and accoutrements for the three hundred thousand men now entering the field had so exhausted the supply that the Thirty-Eighth could not be furnished at once. A few muskets had been stored with the warden of the penitentiary at Jeffersonville for safekeeping and for an emergency, and these Gen. Anderson gave me an order for. He also gave me authority to purchase cartridge-boxes, canteens, knapsacks, blankets, tents, etc., wherever I could procure them. But he enjoined haste; not a moment was to be lost.

Three days after this interview with Gen. Anderson an aid brought me orders to move at once and take the train at the Louisville & Nashville station that night; whereupon, notwithstanding our unreadiness for the field, we proceeded to obey as best we could. Leaving Maj. Merriweather in charge of the camp to receive recruits expected to arrive, we started with 750 men upon the hazardous undertaking, meeting upon the road the wagons with our knapsacks which I had purchased from the manufacturer, who said he had made them for the Kentucky militia. The column was halted and the men supplied. While pursuing our way to the ferry we were met in the street by a delegation of citizens and presented with a beautiful stand of colors, and before the boat left the dock a patriotic citizen handed me an elegant brace of revolving pistols. Arriving at the station in Louisville we drew ammunition, which had to be carried in our pockets, we having no cartridge-boxes or other equipment, except muskets and knapsacks. But the situation was critical; invasion threatened our homes, and war with all its horrors was at our very thresholds. Buckner was reported on his way to Louisville with a large force. All there was to resist him was the Louisville Legion, composed of two regiments and Capt. Stone's battery, commanded by Gen. Lovell H. Rousseau; the Sixth Indiana Volunteers, Col. Thomas Crittenden; the Forty-ninth

Ohio, Col. Gibson; the Thirty-ninth Indiana, Col. Harrison, and two companies of United States Infantry, commanded by Capt. P. T. Swaine. These troops had gone forward a few days before, under the command of Gen. W. T. Sherman. At 7:30 the next morning we arrived at Lebanon Junction, Ky. The ground was strewn with the debris of the camp, and the rear of the column was just leaving. Upon inquiring for Gen. Sherman, a plainly-dressed man in citizen's clothes, wearing a broad-brimmed, well-worn black hat, was pointed out to me as the man. He was approached while he was engaged in hurrying up the tardy ones into the column. The general was informed that I was ordered by Gen. Anderson to report to him for duty. In response he ordered me to fall in with the column now moving, that "he was making a forward movement." I replied that my men had had no breakfast, that we wanted to draw rations at Louisville, but was told that he would supply me. He rejoined: "That's bad; my stores are all packed up and on the road, but everything here belongs to the United States, and you belong to the United

States; so look about and help yourselves to anything you find." We found a barrel of onions and some crackers near the bottom of some boxes and barrels which I presume the men had no room for in their haversacks, but we found no meat or coffee. As my men had no haversacks, the capacity of their pockets and the quantity found were both factors in estimating the amount of supplies obtained. Thus provided we took up our line of march toward Elizabethtown, arriving at the Rolling Fork of Salt river, where we found the bridge had been destroyed and therefore had to ford it waist deep. Gen. Sherman superintended personally the operation. He said to the men: "Take off your shoes and stockings, then put on your shoes again to protect your feet from injury, and after you cross over, drain the water from your shoes, put on your dry socks and you will find it much better than to march with wet feet." This good advice was not forgotten. Crossing over Muldraugh's Hill we entered Elizabethtown about dusk, putting to flight some four hundred of the enemy's cavalry, and bivouacked at the fair grounds, near the town.

The Thirty-eighth went supperless to bed, without even the comfort of a blanket.

The next morning I observed some disorder in the camp, and sought Gen. Sherman, and informed him that some Union citizens, in mistaken kindness, had brought whisky to the men. At this the General flew into a furious rage and ordered me to take my regiment out of the "infernal hole." With much embarrassment, I desired to know the order of march and the direction. "Never mind the order of march; get out the way you came, regardless of the movements of anybody." As we approached the town we came to a road crossing the one from the fair grounds and were much bewildered, not knowing whether to turn to the right or left. I halted the column at being accosted by a citizen, who, pointing to a stage-coach and hack filled with people about to depart from the door of the tavern, earnestly protested against my allowing them to depart, "they were all secessionists and would carry information to Buckner." Capt. Prime, of Sherman's staff, here dashed up and directed to the right, which I proceeded to take, turning the citizen over to him. We soon observed that the whole force followed in the same road. At Muldraugh's Hill, we halted, according to orders, and would have stacked arms, but the Thirty-eighth had not yet reached the training and skill required to perform so intricate a movement. The dinner question was now becoming a most serious and absorbing one. This was especially so with the Thirty-eighth, for they were without either supper or breakfast. My quartermaster, John R. Cannon, was just the man for the place, "alive all over," with a presence and tone of command that a major general might have envied. He soon provided us with an abundance of beef. Having no cooking utensils, we were reduced to the primitive way of roasting it before the fire, which was done in large pieces, and portions from the outside cut off as they became sufficiently cooked. Salt was in demand, but only limited quantities could be obtained by the men from houses in the neighborhood; so we lived by beef alone until the men learned to punch with a nail, holes in a tin plate, making a grater by which meal could be made from the corn now beginning to harden in the fields near by. We had hardly finished our repast when the long roll was heard calling us to arms; fences were thrown down and the battery came swooping down to a position for action; our lines were formed for immediate battle, expecting the enemy to come charging down upon us. Hour after hour we waited, and thus the remainder of the day was spent. That night Gen. Sherman sent for me to report in person to his headquarters, which was a double log-house near at hand. On arriving there I found assembled Gen. Rousseau, Col. Harrison and Capt. Swaine. After the door was closed, Gen. Sherman addressed us in these words, forming his sentences after issuing the smoke of the cigar which he held in his mouth: "Gentlemen, I sent for you to tell you what I know, for what I know I think you ought to know. The enemy, with a force greater than we can hope to overcome, is within a few hours of us. We have no means of transportation to get away, if we were so disposed. The political aspect of affairs in

Kentucky makes it necessary that a stand should be made; so I sent for you to tell you to make up your minds to die right here, and we will fight them down to the stubs. You can retire to your quarters." Without another word the company dispersed. It may be easily imagined that this one-sided council of war did not lull me to pleasant dreams.

Early the next morning I repaired again to the log-cabin and as soon as Gen. Sherman would receive me I had my say. I referred the general to what he had said last night, and felt it due to him and to myself that he should know the condition of my regiment. We were hurried from our camp of organization without cartridge boxes, canteens, haversacks, blankets, tents or wagons; the regiment had not been in line after their muskets were received until they formed to march to the railroad station to join him, and I thought he ought to know this to enable him to justly estimate his available force. Notwithstanding these drawbacks, I assured him that the material of which my command was composed was of the highest character; they "were somebody's sons," and all that men in such a condition could do they would do. The general put his hand on my shoulder approvingly, but without speaking. I continued in some hesitation, in doubt of the propriety of what I intended to say:

"I served in the Mexican War and know with great chagrin what it is to be commanded by incompetent officers. You will doubtless form your command in brigades. Now, may I ask you to place me under the orders of some soldier, one who knows more than I do, one who could get us out of trouble should we get into it. I will obey such an officer if he be but a second lieutenant as faithfully as I would were he a brigadier general. I beg of you not to put me under some of these volunteer colonels, who do not know as much as I do."

The general seemed interested, and I may say pleased, and said that I showed a commendable spirit, and that my wishes should be regarded.

I had closely observed Capt. Swaine, and was much impressed with his style and bearing, and it was he I had in my mind for a commander. It must be borne in mind that the emergency seemed great and that a deadly conflict was hourly expected. But Buckner did not come. I have often since been perplexed to know the reason why he neglected to profit by such a golden opportunity, all things for a successful march upon Louisville seeming so favorable. At one of our army reunions I spoke to Gen. Sherman about it. The general said that he felt the same way, and that he had once asked Buckner why he did not take Louisville at this time, and that Buckner replied that he wanted to but Sidney Johnston would not let him.

It will be remembered that soon after the incidents above described, the wise men at Washington discovered that the mind of Gen. Sherman had become impaired, because, when asked his opinion as to the force that would be required to maintain this line, he replied "Two hundred thousand men." As wild as this estimate seemed to the War Department, they found as the war progressed that Gen. Sherman's head was not so wrong, and the General's mind improved more and more as they found this out. The fame of this great soldier continued to grow until the civilized world was filled with admiration and wonder at his brilliant achievements.

While speaking of Gen. Sherman, I will refer to one of his peculiar traits. His memory of details, of faces, of names and of seemingly unimportant events and circumstances was extraordinary in one whose mind was so engrossed upon great subjects and absorbing cares, and to illustrate this, I will relate an incident which occurred some two years later than that of the log cabin, it being the first time I had had an opportunity to talk with him since. During the Atlanta campaign I had been engaged in a terrible fight at night and was retired with my brigade to the rear to rest, when Gen. Sherman with his staff and other officers rode up and dismounting reclined about on the grass near my fly. During a desultory conversation which ensued, the general turned abruptly to me and asked: "How many men did you kill last night?" Somewhat disturbed by the question, I replied that it was too dark to count the dead, but we brought off some prisoners, many of whom were wounded; and among them several officers. The general interrupted me with, "Never mind the wounded; I want to know how many you killed," then turning to the company, "for I tell you, gentlemen, that there are three hundred thousand of them who will have to be killed before we will have permanent peace in this country." I rejoined aside, for his own ear:

"I suppose, then, we will have to fight them down to the stubs?" He promptly replied, for me alone, "And I suppose that you still want to be commanded by a soldier, one that knows more than you do?" thus showing that he remembered the interview at Muldraugh's Hill.

But to return to the thread of my story. Fears of Buckner subsided, and supplies having come forward, we moved on to Bacon Creek, Ky., where we joined other forces and were formed into brigades: the Thirty-ninth Indiana under Col. Thos. Harrison, the Twenty-ninth under Col. John F. Miller, and the Thirtieth under Col. S. S. Bass, who was afterward killed at Shiloh, and these regiments, together with the Thirty-eighth Indiana, were placed under command of Gen. Thos. J. Wood. Gen. A. McD. McCook commanded the division.

Gov. Morton sent me, in exchange for muskets, Enfield rifles for four companies, and also provided us with gum blankets and other articles which were difficult to obtain at that time from the United States quartermasters. The gratitude of all Indiana soldiers is due Gov. Morton for his constant and earnest care of them during the war. We now set to work to acquire the discipline and knowledge of tactics and army regulations, and much progress was made. But soon a serious drawback impeded our advancement — the typhoid fever broke out in the camp, and prostrated many.

The plan of organizing brigades from troops of the same State was soon very wisely abandoned. The tendency of such a policy was to destroy the national spirit and to cultivate instead, all the heresies of State rights, pride and envy. The Thirty-eighth was transferred to the Seventh Brigade, commanded by Gen. James S. Negley. This command was composed of the Seventy-eighth Pennsylvania, Col. Wm. Sirwell; the Seventy-ninth Pennsylvania, Col. H.

A. Hambright; the First Wisconsin, Col. John Starkweather, and the Thirty-eighth Indiana.

From Bacon Creek McCook's division advanced to Green river, and was at once occupied in repairing the bridge that had been destroyed and in constructing defenses. Upon the arrival of the Thirty-eighth, we were sent across the river to support the pickets, who had been attacked by a regiment of Texas cavalry commanded by Col. Terry, but the fight was over before we got there. The Texans were severely handled and repulsed by Col. Willich's German regiment, the Thirty-second Indiana. The colonel was temporarily absent at the time, and credit for the skillful management of the engagement is due to Lieut.-Col. Von Trebra, who, after some hard fighting, drove the enemy back, killing many of them, among whom was Col. Terry. The disastrous defeat of this crack regiment had quite a moral effect upon both armies. Terry's men had assumed, with much ostentation and arrogance, a superiority over their comrades, and would show off their skill in horsemanship at break-neck speed through the streets of Bowling Green. They boasted, according to a prevailing opinion in the South at this time, "that one southern man could whip five northern men"; so when, crest-fallen and used-up, they returned to their camp, they were met with taunts by their humbler comrades, "Whipped by the Dutch!" They never regained their prestige.

Daily drills continued, and officers' schools were established; heavy details were made to work on the bridge and fortifications, and every seventh day the regiment was detailed to do picket duty across the river. The winter was a severe one, the roads almost impassable, in places over knee-deep with mud, or rather thin clay mortar. After returning from picket, or excursions for wood and straw, or from work on the forts, the men would wade into the ponds, peculiar to this locality, to wash the mud from their garments, after which they would stand before the camp fires to dry, or turn in together in their tents with their wet clothes on. Of course, the officers did all they could to mitigate these evils. The sickness which broke out at Camp Bacon Creek continued, reinforced by the measles. For some time the health of the

Thirty-eighth had been much better than that of the other regiments in the brigade, which fact I attributed to the efficiency of my medical staff. Deep ditches had been dug around the tents and along the company streets to drain off the dampness from the tents and reduce the mud which everywhere prevailed. One day while felicitating my surgeon, Dr. W. A. Clapp, upon the sanitary condition of the regiment, he reversed the flow of my spirits by the statement that he had just finished enumerating the men in the Thirty-eighth who had not had the measles, and found the number to be over four hundred, and he added that they would all have it. This prediction proved only too true! I can recall but few more discouraging scenes than the crowds that assembled daily in front of the doctor's tent at the sick call. As one means of diverting the minds of the men at this time, I ordered a large foot-ball, which would be hurled among the men then assembled so as to arouse in them some interest in life. This was a trying time for both officers and men. Many were discouraged, and many utterly disheartened; complaints, mutterings and even threats prevailed. Only those who have passed through ordeals of this kind can appreciate the difficulties and trials of one in command of troops in such a state. I believe that at one time many could have been found, and amongst them some officers, who would have given up and gone home, so utterly desperate and hopeless was the outlook. I had passed through a similar state of things in Mexico and could assure the men that these clouds would pass away and that the sun would shine for us again, but I could not say as Aeneas did to his comrades when wrecked on the coast of Carthage: "Perchance the time may come when the memory of even this will be a pleasure." I will not speak for others, but, in recalling my experiences during the war, I do not think that we ever encountered anything that would make these times seem pleasant.

On the 13th of February we had the additional mortification of seeing the division of Gen. O. M. Mitchell pass over the bridge we had, with so much labor and hardship, constructed. Weary of the monotony of camp life, we had longed for marching orders; Buckner was at Bowling

Green, our objective point, and we were eager and restive to move upon him. However, the next day marching orders came, but not for this direction. During the day Grant's victory at Fort Henry was known; the gossips said that we were on our way to the Ohio river, there to take boat to join Grant in the assault on Fort Donelson. We bivouacked at night at Upton's Station in a snow storm; the weather was cold and the roads dreadful. The next morning Grant had taken Fort Donelson, and we returned, passing through our camp at Green river, crossed the bridge and moved on to Bowling Green and camped near the fortification of the rebels on the east bank of the Barren river. Buckner had evacuated Bowling Green and had destroyed the bridges. Three days were consumed in constructing means to cross the river, which was flooded by the rains of the season. On March the 5th we marched through Nashville with flags floating and bands playing. Not a pleasing sight for the disappointed citizens to behold! We rested for several days at Camp Andy Johnson, some five miles out of the city.

After the fall of Fort Donelson, the news was soon spread in Nashville, and the wildest excitement was created thereby, which can be best comprehended by those who lived near the border or on the route which Morgan took when he invaded Indiana and Ohio. The panic reached its climax on Sunday morning during church services. The congregations were dismissed, and the men, without distinction or favor, were pressed into service by the authorities and were set at work unloading steamboats, loading wagons, etc., in order that property might be saved from falling into our hands. Many ludicrous scenes were described by the Union men who came about us at this time, and much valuable information was given us by them.

About this time I was detailed by Gen. Buell as president of a board, consisting of three officers, to determine whether the vast quantities of stores which fell into our hands at the fall of Nashville were private or public property. Gen. Buell issued a proclamation declaring that private property should be restored, and only property belonging to the Confederate Government should be seized. Accordingly, many questions arose as to what was private and what public property. I was employed several days upon this business, and had some new and interesting experiences. To illustrate the state of things in Nashville at this time, and to show how some men will act when pressed by adversity, in order to frustrate an enemy, a few examples are here given. One day a gentleman called at the office of the board and asked for the presiding officer, and after an introduction of himself and complimentary references to the board, he continued:

"I am a lawyer by profession, and an old citizen of Nashville. I have a young friend who was born in the city and whom I have known all his life; he is poor, and what he has, he has earned by his work, and that little your people have taken from him and if he loses it, he loses his all."

The gentleman was assured that the government of the United States did not intend to be unjust, or to seize private property from private citizens. He was rejoiced to hear me speak in this way and, in compliance with my request, said he would send the young man to us, with the assurance that a great wrong would be righted. When the young man presented himself and the nature of his claim was asked, he offered a paper, of which the following is the purport. It is not pretended that it is an accurate copy; I do not now remember the young man's name, but the impression the paper would give is correct.

NASHVILLE, TENN., February 13th, 1862.

Mr....................
Bought of E. M. Bruce & Co.

2000 sides of bacon..	$ 20,000
1000 hams...	12,000
1000 shoulders...	11,000
	$ 43,000

Received payment, E. M. Bruce & Co.

The young man stated that this was the property our forces had seized. I was greatly shocked at the audacity of this claim. We had, while examining other claims, discovered that E. M. Bruce & Co. were contractors; the Confederate Government had furnished them the money to buy the hogs, and they delivered to the proper authorities the six pieces, the two hams, two shoulders and the two sides, and retained the balance of the hog for their compensation. This fact, and the date of the transaction, it being at the time of the panic, rendered the case a very simple one. But, in order to bring out all the facts of this intended fraud, and to afford the young man a chance to explain, an opportunity was given him to do so. He was told that we were informed that his means were limited, yet this bill seemed to us a very large one for a poor man to pay. He spoke up and said, "I did not pay it all down." After much persistence, we were able to find that only seven hundred dollars were paid down and that the balance was paid by giving his unindorsed note at twelve months' time without interest, and the seven hundred dollars were paid in Confederate notes, which had now been much reduced in value, and it was desirable to get rid of them at a great sacrifice. But I need not pursue this case further.

Breastworks had been constructed of cotton bales to protect a certain point from our gunboat, and when the rebels evacuated the place, they set fire to the cotton. The fire was extinguished by our men, and yet claim for this cotton was made with much persistence.

A large foundry employed in making cannon and projectiles, with large quantities of cannon and pig iron on hand, had been seized by our forces, and claim for the restoration of this property was set up under Buell's proclamation. We cut this case off without much delay and held the property as contraband of war. Large quantities of pig iron were found along the river bank, after the high water subsided. It had been thrown overboard on that exciting day. We had a good claim to this iron, from the fact that files of the city newspapers showed that the Confederate authorities had advertised that iron would be considered as delivered if placed anywhere along the bank of the river in front of the city. But I will not stop to detail the various grounds and evidence we were in possession of to show the effrontery of many of the claims set up at this time.

The Seventh Brigade was transferred from McCook's division to that of Gen. Mitchell, and when Gen. Buell, with the rest of the army, moved to reinforce Grant at Shiloh, Gen. Negley returned to the work of building roads, bridges and stockades, with the occasional diversion of trying to overtake and capture cavalry with infantry. About the first of April, I was assigned to the command of the post at Shelbyville, Tenn., with the Thirty-eighth and the Twenty-first Kentucky, under Col. Price. It was refreshing to be thrown with loyal, hospitable and refined people again; it was to us like an oasis in the desert. On May 10, with the Thirty-eighth, I joined Gen. Negley at Pulaski, Tenn., who, with two brigades, was about to make a raid through middle and southern Tennessee and northern Alabama. We made long and difficult marches in various directions, and at length reached the Tennessee river at Rogersville after a march that day of thirty miles. A rebel brigade, under Gen. Adams, was here encountered and driven across the river, leaving twenty of their dead, and with an aggregate loss of sixty. After a few hours' rest, at 7 P. M. the same day we started for Florence, Ala., and arrived there at daylight the next morning, having marched twenty-one miles, and making fifty-one miles in a single day. We forded swollen streams whose turbulent currents, obstructed by the wrecked bridges, roared like rushing torrents. The native "Whip-poor-wills" from their homes in the forest joined in the concert with their rhythmical cadences augmenting the sense of loneliness which pervaded our spirits like a weird and ghastly wilderness. At times the shadows of the trees in the moonlight so obstructed the road that it was difficult to find our way, and it was unsafe to halt the column to rest, lest the men, overcome with sleep, would be left behind when the march was resumed. Many were the expedients resorted to by the officers to interest and amuse the men as they trudged along, to keep them awake and to prevent them from dropping down by the roadside overcome by fatigue and sleep. We found no enemy at Florence; if any were there, they were mounted, and could easily elude us; but the main object of the expedition was accomplished in confusing the enemy as to where Union forces were located and in retarding the operations of guerrillas, who were prowling about the country, and also we were co-operating with the plans of the commanding general. Having rested all day, in the evening we started on our return to Columbia, *via* Tuscumbia and Decatur, thus making a march of 207 miles in ten days.

On the 20th of May, Gen. Negley's command again took the war path. The Ninth Michigan, under Col. Parkhurst, together with the Thirty-eighth Indiana, was called a brigade, to the command of which I was assigned. We crossed the western range of the Cumberland mountains at Cowan, and descended at Sweden's Cove, where our advance had a skirmish in which thirty of the enemy were killed and wounded. Having crossed Waldron's ridge, we formed a line on the bank of the Tennessee river opposite Chattanooga. Some shells from our batteries were fired upon a few rebel soldiers to be seen, but they did not return the fire with artillery. We were, however, within range of their small arms, and a desultory firing was kept up for several hours. Toward evening Gen. Negley recrossed Waldron's ridge, leaving my command as rear guard to protect and assist the trains over the mountains. The ascent of Waldron's ridge is steep and crooked, the road much of the way is composed of logs, one end of which rest on the side of the mountain, the other end supported in a horizontal position by props, thus forming a sort of corduroy road. At one point near the summit a stream of water ran down the mountain's side through the interstices of the logs. It was a rickety, insecure makeshift of a road, and was so narrow that only in places could two teams pass each other. On looking up at the zigzag way, the wagons appeared in terraces one line above another, and one above could look down upon the tops of huge trees which grew in great luxuriance. It was yet daylight when the train started up the ascent, and such disposition of the two regiments was made as would best protect it. The proximity of the enemy and the nature of the road increased the danger, as even a small force could inflict great damage by stampeding the mules in so precarious a situation. At length the train ceased to move, and one staff officer after another was sent forward to ascertain the cause. The wagons ahead had stalled, night and darkness came on, detail after detail from the troops was made to assist the teams until all of both regiments had gone forward for this duty, and it was midnight when I reached the summit, myself alone comprising the rear guard, for I preferred to stay behind the wagons rather than to venture upon the passage of the wagons on the verge of such a yawning abyss. The Thirty-eighth returned to Shelbyville *via* Altamont, Manchester and Wartrace, having marched 317 miles in thirteen days. The heat, dust, frequent alarms and consequent deployment of the column, the constant watchfulness required, all conspired to make the march one of the most fatiguing we ever made. We were perplexed with reports that the enemy was lying in wait for us here and there, and frequently skirmishes and double-quick movements for position became necessary. The wear and tear on clothes and shoes on this expedition was great, and at times the men suffered some discomfort from these causes; but Gen. Negley was very considerate and efficient in such matters, and either carried such supplies in his train, or had them sent to us at points pre-arranged. I understood that the object of this expedition was to hinder reinforcements for Beauregard.

OFF TO WAR AND THE FIGHT BEGINS. 49

The battle of Shiloh had been fought and won, and Gen. Buell's army was expected east to occupy Chattanooga, and we supposed that to favor these movements we were thus employed by Gen. Mitchell.

The Thirty-eighth made another hard march about this time. Gen. Negley had a large train of supplies on the way to Winchester, Tenn. Lieut. J. V. Kelso, a painstaking and capable officer, quartermaster of the Thirty-eighth, was in charge of it. The General received information that guerrillas designed to attack it; so he despatched a courier to Kelso, ordering him to hold the train at a cross-road six miles from Tullahoma, and there await an escort. The Thirty-eighth was detailed for this duty, and set out upon a march of thirty-five miles. The day was hot, and the dust and scarcity of water caused the men to suffer beyond description. Approaching the long-desired haven of rest, the comforting intelligence was sent to the tired men: "Only two miles to camp"; and then, after an interval, "only one mile to camp"; and in every way I strove to encourage the poor fellows to drag one foot after another. At length the ever seemingly receding place of rest was reached. It was a beautiful spot, covered with grass and shaded with an alluring grove of trees. A stream of running water bubbled and laughed as it ran along, as if to welcome and invite the men to bathe and refresh their weary bodies. But it was not to be; the courier failed to meet the train and it had passed on to Tullahoma an hour before we reached the place of meeting. Here was a dilemma. It was my duty to follow after the train six miles farther. It was a painful thing to do, but there was no help for it; it had to be done; it was done; and well it was, for there was a force hovering about the train, intending to capture it during the night, and perhaps would have made the attempt had it been without protection. But it was a long while before I ceased to hear, "only one mile to camp," repeated by the men; they rung all the changes upon it, and afterward, when nearing the end of a long march, or when they thought it was time to stop, the phrase would be taken up and repeated along the line. But I assured the boys that I did not intend to deceive them, and really thought that it was but a mile to camp.

On June 23, 1862, Gen. Negley went upon another march, this time our route lying through Huntsville, Athens, Shellmound, Stevenson, Ala., and Battle Creek. Here the army of the Cumberland assembled, and many changes in its organization were made. Gen. Rousseau relieved Gen. Mitchell of the command of the third division, whereupon I wrote the following letter to Gen. Rousseau, to-wit:

HEADQUARTERS, THIRTY-EIGHTH INDIANA VOLUN-
TEERS, BATTLE CREEK, AUGUST 10, 1862.

My Dear General:

Presuming upon our long acquaintance and the fact of our having passed through Buena Vista's fiery ordeal together, I feel that I may speak freely to you as a fellow soldier and friend. It has been intimated to me that my regiment would be one of those left to guard this place when the main body marches. Now, while I do not underrate the importance of such duty, I feel that, in view of my long service in this capacity, I may with propriety protest against its again falling to my lot. You doubtless remember the circumstances of my entering the service; how my command was hurried off without accoutrements, and pressed forward with your column to Elizabethtown, and shared your hardships and privations at Muldraugh's Hill. In view of this, may I not ask you for an honorable position in the first line of the Army of the Ohio? I am convinced that any talents or acquirements I may possess are better suited to operations in the field than to scouting for bushwhackers or pursuing guerrillas. I desire to march with the column; to go with the through train, and not to be switched off on the side-track. I beg your influence and aid to accomplish this desire. Will you please transfer me to such portions of your line as are sure to go forward, or, if this be impossible, represent in such a manner to the commanding general as will secure this coveted position, and thereby render me, Ever yours,

(Signed) B. F. SCRIBNER.

A few days after this letter was written, an order by telegraph came from Gen. Buell assigning the Thirty-eighth to the Ninth Brigade, commanded by Col. Sill, afterward Gen. Sill, who gallantly fell at the battle of Stone River.

Bragg, with a large force, occupied the opposite side of the river from Battle Creek. Each army had constructed fortifications, and rifle pits were dug near the edge of the river. Much chaff and badinage passed to and fro between the men, for the river was low and the distance short. On the evening of the 17th of August, orders were received to move with the Thirty-eighth on the following morning, at three o'clock, via Sweden's Cove, to Decherd, Tenn. We were cautioned to do this quietly, without any noise or stir that would excite the suspicion of the enemy. We accordingly proceeded on a familiar march, undergoing the hardships already described. I must confess that climbing mountains was becoming a little monotonous. Upon our arrival at Decherd I was assigned to the command of the post. My orders were to fortify the place and picket all roads leading to it, and to use every precaution against a surprise. An inkling of the situation now began to dawn on me. Bragg had crossed the Tennessee river and was reported to be moving north. On the 25th Gen. Buell and staff arrived and remained several days. He sent for me to inquire about the roads on the mountains and the possibility of handling large bodies of troops upon them. Upon this point I could speak advisedly for I had had experience on the mountains. Decherd had now assumed much importance; large quantities of stores were accumulated there, and troops and trains filled the roads both day and night, passing northward. We now had another brigade commander, Col. Sill having been transferred to another command. He was succeeded by Col. Len. Harris, of the Second Ohio. He with the brigade, excepting the Thirty-eighth, had been left at Battle Creek, to bring off the rear of the army. The enemy, prematurely for Col. Harris, became aware of Buell's movements, and vigorously assailed him with shell and solid shot from their batteries on the opposite side of the river, and the Colonel suffered some loss in drawing off his force. Upon his arrival at Decherd the Ninth Brigade was together again.

Buell's retrograde was now developed, and we joined in the march for Louisville, unless a collision with Bragg should occur on the way, as he was heading in the same direction. It was regarded as a race between Buell and Bragg for Louisville. It was a very fatiguing and dispiriting march; the dust and heat on the crowded road were excessive, the season of the year and the great demand making water very scarce. Telegraph wires were cut, bridges destroyed, stockades and water tanks demolished, and so we trudged along. It was especially painful and humiliating to pass our former camps and witness the destruction of works we had with so much labor and hardship constructed. Not far from our old camp at Green river we saw the troops who had been captured and paroled by Bragg at the bridge we had built at Green river. Their dejected faces filled us with pity and indignation. They repeatedly refused to surrender to the demands from Bragg, and did so only after their commander had personally been shown the rebel army by which they were surrounded. Even then they demanded honorable terms and marched out with their side arms and personal effects. Bragg granted these liberal terms because he did not wish to attract Buell's attention, and also to save the time that a siege would entail. My personal discomfort on this march was excessive. I had taken what was said to be a summer cold, which so effected my eyes that the light could not be borne without great distress, sneezing, coughing and wheezing from asthma attending me day and night during the march. It was not known then, nor was it decided until two years later, that it was hay fever that was afflicting me, and each succeeding year from that time to this it has returned with wonderful punctuality.

At length we reached the Ohio river at

West Point, Ky., twenty miles below Louisville, and, as we proceeded up the river road, many of my men could look across the river and behold their homes which, for twelve long, lagging months, they had so wistfully yearned for. They could see the houses in which they were born and around which clustered the associations of their youth. About the doors and yards were gathered women and children, answering their cheers with handkerchiefs and flags. It was a rare and touching sight to see these poor fellows so covered with the limestone dust that their garments, beards, hair and visages were all of the same color, all seeming old and gray with the dust and bending under the burden of their guns and knapsacks, limping along with their blistered feet. They appeared more like grim spectres than young and sturdy men, whose hearts were beating with tenderness and love for the dear ones they were thus passing by without a word or caress. After another night of travel, this memorable march of three hundred miles was ended, and early on the morning of the 26th of September, 1862, we arrived at Louisville. Buell had won the race and occupied Louisville.

Bragg was outside, but whether he would stay out, was yet to be decided. Four days were consumed in resting and refitting the men. Many recruits and new regiments were added to Buell's army, and among them were those who under Gen. Nelson at Richmond, Ky., had a few days before been so disastrously overpowered and routed. One of these, the Ninety-fourth Ohio Volunteers, Col. Frizell, joined the Ninth Brigade. The Fifth Indiana Battery, under Capt. P. Simmonson, was also assigned to us. Col. Len. Harris commanded the brigade, Gen. Lovell H. Rousseau the division, and A. McD. McCook the corps, and Gen. Buell the army.

On October the 1st we commenced the movement upon Bragg, who was reported at Bardstown, Ky. McCook passed through Taylorsville, Gen. Gilbert through Shepherdsville and Gen. Thomas L. Crittenden through Mount Washington, on roads leading to Bardstown. On the 7th we passed through Mackville. The day's march was increased three miles from difficulties in getting water, the season being a very dry one and water scarce. We moved early on the morning of the 8th, having been careful to fill our canteens with water, for there was none this side of Chaplin Creek. The enemy occupied Perryville and was so posted as to deprive us of water. A desultory firing was heard at the front, and our pace was quickened.

About noon the column was halted, and I rode forward a short distance and joined Gen. Rousseau, who was sitting on a log on the roadside; but soon cannonading was heard and I hastened back to my regiment. On the way a cannon ball came whizzing by me and bounded along the road. We were faced to the front, and the Thirty-third Ohio was deployed as skirmishers, and a brisk fire of musketry ensued. The Thirty-eighth was moved about to several positions, and at length was, with the Tenth Wisconsin, hurried up the road to the support of a battery which was in position near a house on the road, and we moved into position under a heavy fire. The battery which we were to support limbered up and withdrew, and its place was taken by our own battery under Capt. Simmonson. In a very few minutes he was ordered away by the chief of artillery, having lost in killed fourteen men and sixteen horses. We were moved forward to a slight elevation or ridge, where we were partially protected. Three batteries of the enemy concentrated their fire upon us and three times their infantry advanced upon us, but each time they were repulsed and fell back. We occupied this position for two hours and a half, the men taking deliberate aim and appearing to be as cool as if on drill. Having exhausted their forty rounds of cartridges, they proceeded to use those in the boxes of the killed and wounded, and when none were left they fixed bayonets and awaited orders. It was of vital importance that our line should be held, for the flank of Gen. Lytle on our right would have been turned had the enemy passed on through a gap made by our withdrawal. As it was, Lytle did not join us, but was some distance off on the same general line. Lytle, however, was soon forced to fall back, but in good order, notwithstanding the terrific fire to which he was subjected. This exposed our right, which the enemy took advantage of, and had moved up a battery to enfilade us and, therefore, being without ammunition, we were wisely ordered back out of range of the enemy's missiles, where we lay down to await the wagon with ammunition. The battle was now renewed with great fury, and to my consternation there came down upon us a fleeing mob of routed and panic-stricken raw recruits, who, rushing in a disorganized mass, with the enemy at their heels and trampling over my men, fled away like scared sheep. I was in utter despair, and thought that all was lost, expecting of course that the Thirty-eighth would be swept away with the crowd, but to my surprise and joy, there lay my brave boys; not a man was missed, and springing to their feet, with bayonets fixed and without a round of ammunition, they were prepared to sell their lives dearly. The Twenty-second Indiana had moved up on my right. I dashed up to the field officer on their left and pointing out the enemy's advancing line, urged him to open upon them a well directed fire, which they did, and which seemed to check their advance. The men were urged to continue their fire, and the effect of their shot was magnified, to encourage them to keep it up; and thus we escaped destruction. I owe a debt of gratitude to this gallant regiment who, fresh from the honorable field of Pea Ridge, here gained fresh laurels. But with what terms of praise could I express my feelings to my brave fellows. With tears of joy I could have hugged them all. Only those who have had something like this occur to them can know how I felt and will ever feel to those heroes. Ammunition was at length distributed, and we moved to the support of a battery, and this position was maintained until the close of the day ended the conflict. The Thirty-eighth went into the fight with only five hundred men, lost twenty-seven killed, one hundred and twenty-three wounded, and seven captured, the latter being taken after the battle and at night while searching for wounded comrades, and for water, they having wandered within the enemy's lines. This shows a loss of over thirty per cent. The severity of this engagement may be appreciated by the fact that of the nine men who composed the color guard, five were killed, the color-bearer wounded in two places, two had their clothes penetrated by bullets, thus leaving but one unscathed. The flag was riddled almost into shreds, the top of the staff being shot away, and two balls struck the staff, causing it to break, after the battle, at these places. I was struck near the knee-joint by a spent ball, which only broke the skin, and my horse was shot in the neck, but his windpipe was not injured and he at length got well, but with an altered disposition, for instead of being fearless and indifferent to the noise of artillery or small arms, he would ever after sigh, buck and balk and manifest great alarm and uneasiness in battle.

The health of Col. Harris was so broken that soon after the battle he was forced to resign, and I was assigned to the command of the brigade. Lieut.-Col. Walter Q. Gresham had resigned in December, 1861, to accept the colonelcy of the Fifty-Third Indiana, and Maj. Merriweather was promoted lieutenant-colonel. On September 3, 1862, he resigned, Adjt. D. F. Griffin becoming major, and was now lieutenant-colonel commanding the regiment— Capt. John B. Glover, commanding Company D., becoming major and George H. Devol, adjutant.

But to continue: Bragg fell back toward Danville and, after burying our dead and caring for our wounded, we moved after him and pursued him to Crab Orchard, and the advance followed him until he took to the mountains.

Buell was soon after superseded by Gen. W. S. Rosecrans. There has been much criticism and discussion concerning the wisdom and policy of Gen. Buell's actions. It is not to be expected that from my position I should know much about this, but I incline to the opinion that his plans of the battle with Bragg were wisely made, and, had not the conflict been brought on before his troops were in position, Bragg's army would have been destroyed. But it is often so; the enemy sometimes will not wait until a mathematical certainty is assured. This much I will here say, that notwithstanding his coldness and austerity of manner and seeming indifference to the private soldier and distrust of volunteers, the Army of the Cumberland owe much to Gen. Buell for their discipline and education in the forms and technique of the profession of arms. Much ridicule was made of red tape, but while it will not supply the place of enterprise and pluck, still there is the foundation of reason and propriety in it.

CHAPTER III.

ANOTHER BATTLE.

HAVING spent a few days at Crab Orchard, the army moved toward Nashville. Near Bowling Green we met our new commander, Gen. Rosecrans, who addressed us with much warmth and good-will. He made a favorable impression upon the men by his open and genial manner, contrasting agreeably with the taciturn exclusiveness of Gen. Buell, whom but a very few of the men had ever seen. My command was stationed for a time at Edgefield Junction, and was ordered to make a reconnoissance to Springfield, Tenn., and adjacent country. It was reported that large quantities of stores had been collected there for Bragg's army. I sent the Second Ohio and Thirty-eighth Indiana regiments on this duty, and they brought in and forwarded to the proper authorities at Nashville two thousand barrels of flour, four thousand pounds of bacon and twenty-five barrels of whisky. From the scarcity of salt in the Confederacy, or from ignorance of packing, or climatic causes, the meat taken from the enemy was unfit to issue to our men, however acceptable it may have been to the poorly-fed Confederates. The dainty appetites of our boys could not be persuaded to accept it. Gen. Robert McFeely, now the efficient commissary-general of the United States, said to me that the bacon turned in by me from Springfield was the only good meat that fell into our hands at that time.

A pleasing incident occurred at this time. The patriotic citizens of New Albany, hearing of the dilapidated condition of the flag of the Thirty-eighth, made them a new one and sent it to them by a committee consisting of Col. E. A. Maginness, my successor in command of the Seventh Regiment of the Indiana Legion, Mr. J. C. Culbertson and Mr. H. N. Devol. After the ceremony and speeches, a suitable banquet was enjoyed, and thus closed an episode prized in the memory of all.

Having reached Nashville, we again found quarters at Camp Andy Johnson, and employed our time in preparation for another campaign. Some changes were made in the designations of the commands by Gen. Rosecrans. The Ninth Brigade was now the First Brigade, First Division, Fourteenth Army Corps, the brigade commanded by me, the division by Gen. Rousseau, and the corps by Gen. Geo. H. Thomas. Gen. A. McD. McCook commanded the right, Gen. Thomas L. Crittenden the left, and Gen. Thomas the center, and on Christmas day the movement on Bragg was commenced. On the 27th we reached Nolinville in the rain. The bad roads and advance troops of the enemy impeded our progress toward the location assumed by Bragg. On the 30th, our skirmishers had developed the position from which Bragg did not intend to retire without a fight, and our line was formed accordingly. On the morning of the 31st, Rousseau in reserve, was massed on the right of the Nashville and Murfreesboro pike in an open field, with our right near a cedar thicket. I will here quote from my official report of this battle, as perhaps the best way to describe it, to-wit:

ANOTHER BATTLE. 67

"HEADQUARTERS FIRST BRIGADE, FIRST DIV., CENTRE
     MURFREESBORO, TENN., JANUARY 9, 1863.

"CAPT. M. C. TAYLOR, A. A. A. G.:

"*Sir*,—I have the honor to submit the following report of the part borne by my command in the engagement before Murfreesboro on the 31st of December and the three succeeding days.

"At daylight we left our bivouac and moved about a mile to the front and formed the second line of your division, two regiments extending into the cedar thicket on the right, and the left extending to the Nashville and Murfreesboro pike. My line was disposed in the following order from right to left, viz.: Tenth Wisconsin, Col. A. R. Chapin; Ninety-fourth Ohio, Col. J. W. Frizel; Thirty-eighth Indiana, Lieut.-Col. D. F. Griffin; Thirty-third Ohio, Capt. E. J. Ellis; Second Ohio, Lieut.-Col. Jno. Kell. Having just finished loading arms, I received your order to proceed in double-quick time to the assistance of the right wing, and to follow the Seventeenth Brigade on the Pioneer road into the woods. When the Seventeenth Brigade halted in the woods, I was ordered by Gen.

Thomas to move to the right, and soon after formed my line of battle near the Wilkinson pike, on the left of Gen. Sheridan, when we were opened upon the enemy's batteries. When near this position, the Thirty-third and Second Ohio regiments were, by your order, detached and moved back near to the position we first occupied, to support our batteries stationed there, and nobly did they defend them, for soon afterward the enemy fiercely charged them and were handsomely repulsed, the Second Ohio capturing the colors of the Thirtieth Arkansas, a victory dearly bought by the loss of the gallant Lieut.-Col. Kell.

" From near the Wilkinson pike I was ordered to move back in great haste to our position on the Nashville pike, to support the batteries, which I at once proceeded to do. My right had just emerged from the woods, when the enemy, who had just been repulsed in their effort to take the batteries before mentioned, were seen retiring in disorder in a northwesterly direction through a narrow neck of woods. They were opened upon by the Ninety-fourth Ohio and two companies of the Thirty-eighth Indiana. I then threw forward my skirmishers and advanced my command about six hundred yards into the woods, where my lines became masked by General Negley's division, which was falling back under a heavy fire from the enemy, who appeared to be advancing from a point south of the direction of the retreating column. I opened my line to permit General Negley to pass, which they did, for they had expended their ammunition. Here the Ninety-fourth Ohio was ordered to the pike, leaving me but two regiments, the Thirty-eighth Indiana and Tenth Wisconsin to form on the right. I soon found myself nearly surrounded, a heavy column turning my left. The Tenth Wisconsin was ordered to change front, forming a right angle with the Thirty-eighth Indiana. This position was scarcely taken when the enemy came down upon us with great fury. They appeared to be massed in several lines and their head seemed to be in terraces not twenty-five yards before us. For twenty minutes these two regiments maintained their ground, completely checking the advance of the enemy's column. Here the Thirty-eighth lost their brave captain, J. E. Fouts, besides nearly one-third of their number in killed and wounded. Lieut.-Col. Griffin and Maj. J. B. Glover both had their horses shot under them and their clothing perforated with bullets. The Tenth Wisconsin nobly vied with their comrades on the right, and I am convinced that both regiments would have suffered extermination rather than yield their ground without orders. But at length the order came and we fell back and formed on the pike, and fronting the cedar thicket, but the enemy did not venture to follow us farther than the edge of the woods.

"Having re-formed my brigade, I advanced my right to the woods from which we had just emerged, deployed, as skirmishers, the Ninety-fourth Ohio through the neck of timber, with my left resting on the Nashville pike. Here we remained the remainder of the day under the fire of sharp-shooters, and ever and anon the shot and shell from the enemy's batteries on our left fell among us. A ball from the former struck Gen. Frizel on the shoulder, so wounding him that he was borne from the field on which he had so nobly performed his duty.

"At four o'clock on the morning of January 1st, you ordered me to take my command back to a point on the pike, near the place we bivouacked before the battle commenced, in order that they might build fires and warm themselves and get something to eat. Upon receiving your caution to protect myself from an attack on the left, and from your allusion to a ford in that direction I ordered Lieut. Alex Martin, inspector, and Lieut. M. Allen, topographical engineer, of my staff, to reconnoiter the place. Upon their reporting the possibility of the crossing, they were ordered to conduct the Second Ohio, under Maj. Anson G. McCook, to the position. Soon after firing was heard in this direction, and a stampede occurred among the wagons and hospitals, and I sent the Tenth Wisconsin to support the Second Ohio, placing them behind the embankment of the railroad. This disposition had just been made, when your order came to hurry to the front again with my command. Having complied with the order, and after some maneuvering, we were placed in position, the Thirty-third Ohio extending across the neck of woods into which my right threw out skirmishers the evening before. A battery on the right and left commanded the fields on either side of the woods; on the right of the Thirty-third was placed the Ninety-fourth Ohio and Thirty-eighth Indiana in the edge of the undergrowth on the crest of the slope from the fields west of the Nashville pike, and on the right of the Thirty-eighth was another battery. The Tenth Wisconsin was held in reserve in order to reinforce any part of the line that was menaced. This important and well chosen position was maintained without material change during the subsequent days of the battle. Our skirmishers were kept out during the time and were employed in discovering and dislodging sharp-shooters, who during the hours of daylight continuously annoyed us. I can not too highly praise Capt. Ellis, commanding the Thirty-third Ohio, for the vigilance of himself and men in their exposed position in the woods. At times the enemy, from the woods below, would essay to advance, when every man would be at his post, and often our batteries would join in their repulse. While here, Capt. Ellis had his horse shot from under him. A breastwork of logs and rocks, had been constructed, and a few rifle pits were dug to protect the line.

"On the evening of the 2d, when the enemy so vigorously attacked our left, the moving of their columns could be seen from my position, which fact was promptly reported, and I caused my skirmishers to advance and took precautions against an attack. The attempt was made just before dark. The enemy formed in the edge of the woods in our front, when Capt. Cox's Tenth Indiana Battery, on the right of the Thirty-third Ohio, opened fire upon them and drove them back.

"I deem it improper to close this report without commending in high terms the manner in which my command bore the hardships of this terrible conflict. They suffered from rain, cold, fatigue and hunger without a murmur. These attributes, when added to their bravery, make soldiers of whom their country may be proud.

"I also deem it proper to praise the courage and efficiency of my staff, Lieut. Fitzwilliam, acting assistant adjutant-general and aid-de-camp; Geo. H. Hollister, acting assistant commissary of subsistence, missing after displaying great gallantry in his intermission of orders, Lieut. M. Allen, topographical engineer; and Lieut. Alex. Martin, who was wounded above the knee at my side by a shell, all of whom endeared themselves to me by their prompt and diligent performance of their appropriate duties.

"I would also, in an especial manner, mention one of my orderlies, Josiah F. Mitchell, Company B, Thirty-third Ohio Volunteers, who displayed marked courage and intelligence.

"I went into the fight with 1,646 men, minus two companies of the Thirty-third Ohio, commanded by Maj. Ely, of the Tenth Wisconsin, who were detached to guard a train. My loss is thirty-two killed, 180 wounded and forty-five missing." I have felt free to thus embody the above report at this place, because in a supplemental report of the battle of Stone river, by Gen. Thomas, my report was approved and largely quoted from by him, and the same was also endorsed and forwarded by Gen. Rosecrans. See reports of the battle of Stone river from the Secretary of War to the United States Senate, March 13, 1863.

But no merely official report of an engagement can adequately represent the conflict which rages within the breasts of those taking part in it. When a great battle has been fought and perchance won, its announcement is received as an accomplished fact; the anxieties and uncertainties pertaining to the actors in it are overlooked in the general rejoicing, and triumph is regarded as a matter of course. But while the conflict is yet undecided, no one can predict the result; that history is being made, that great consequences hang upon the issue may at times be comprehended, but no one knows the end. Life or death, victory or defeat are wavering in the balance; every moment is pregnant with contingencies which may make or mar the wisest plans and fondest hopes.

Every incentive that can influence the actions of man is often required to make him overcome that instinct of nature which prompts him to avoid danger, and to incite and fortify him for the performance of duty. Patriotism, sense of honor, personal and family pride, ambition, fear of disgrace and consequent mortification of friends and loved ones, all may be needed to exalt him to great actions on great occasions. At times constant watchfulness is necessary to enable him to retain control of himself; he may even resort to trivial expedients to steady his nerves; he may count the buttons on a soldier's coat or observe and criticise the condition of his equipment while shot and shell are raining and bursting about him, in order to force and prove to himself that he is calm and self-possessed. "To command others, command yourself," has been wisely said. A marked difference in the duties of the soldier and the officer exists in this. The soldier is occupied with his loading and firing, in estimating his distance and arranging the sights of his gun accordingly, while the officer, surrounded perhaps by the same distracting terrors, must think, must plan, must watch the movements of the enemy and determine whether they are endeavoring to outflank him, or about to move up another battery to bear upon him. These must all be mentally considered under apprehensions of the same deafening roar and bloodshed. I do not believe that men are equally brave at all times. This three-o'clock-in-the-morning courage may exist, but most men, I think, would prefer even a few buttons to count previous to going out before breakfast to be shot at, and there are many instances of troops who have been stampeded, overcome and completely routed, who have afterward behaved like heroes! But the most pitiable object that human nature sometimes exhibits, is the man who, utterly bereft of every instinct of manhood, defeated, dispirited and lost to all sense of shame, has hopelessly given up. He may be pleaded with, threatened or kicked, but like a whipped cur, he will make no defense, and would not lift a finger to save the day, or even to save his own miserable life. I saw some objects like this during the Mexican War, but once in a lifetime will suffice for me. An occasional constitutional coward is met with, who will faint and vomit when scared. Two cases of this kind are the extent of my observation. Courage is not an exceptional quality. In this country it is a national attribute. Americans, as a race, are brave and warlike.

The plans of Rosecrans and Bragg at Stone river seem to have been identical, each general intending to assail the other's right, and had each side been more successful, the anomaly of two armies exchanging lines and cutting each other off from their base of supply might have occurred; but Bragg, with his characteristic dash, took the initiative, and Rosecrans, therefore, was put upon the defensive and had to postpone the execution of his plan. Bragg had massed his forces and came down on McCook like a whirlwind, forcing him to yield position after position until his right had been driven back and became perpendicular with his first position. Thomas, commanding the center, was able, by hard fighting and great loss, to substantially maintain his position. Crittenden, commanding the left wing, was not seriously engaged on the first day, except as he may have sent assistance to the right and center.

As I passed out of the cedars into the open field, after I had given the order from Gen. Rousseau to fall back, I observed Gen. Thomas on the pike to the left of the point at which I had directed my men to re-form. It at once flashed upon my mind what would be Gen. Thomas' impression of the manner my men were told to cross the open field, as if fleeing in disorder to escape the assaults of the enemy, so I dashed up to him and explained that we had been in the cedars, where we were able to hold our own; we were not being driven out, but were acting in obedience to the order of Gen. Rousseau, who directed me to fall back to the pike, and as we looked upon what seemed a panic-stricken route, I added that I had told the men to disperse when they entered the field, and every man for himself, to run for the pike, for the enemy would doubtless pursue and have them at a disadvantage. Then, pointing to the pike, I said, "And now, General, you see they are re-forming." Then, lifting my hat, I asked, "Have you any further orders?" He replied, "No, re-form on the pike." This was the most extended interview I had had with Gen. Thomas, and was the foundation for that good opinion the General ever manifested toward my command.

The night after the first day's fight was a trying one to my command. They maintained all night the line upon which they formed during the afternoon, and, having to lie down upon the wet and muddy ground, their clothes were in a sorry plight. The night turned cold, and many had their garments frozen to the ground. Fires were not permitted, even to boil their coffee. The officers, however, had no difficulty in enforcing this command, for the striking of a match to light a pipe would bring a bullet whizzing by and thus prove the wisdom of the order. The movement of the ambulances and cries for help and water from the wounded, who were strewn over the field, was alone sufficient to drive away all sleep. One poor fellow, not far from me, kept up an incessant cry of "Oh, God Almighty!! God Almighty! God Almighty!!!" I sent a staff officer repeatedly to assist and comfort him, but without avail, for he kept up that piteous wail until the hospital detail bore him off. There is something awful and mournful in death under all circumstances, but with the dead arranged for burial by a professional undertaker there is a calmness, a repose, a dignity, a reverend and subdued tone and order that saddens but does not horrify, but on the battlefield there is a different scene. Here, as at some vast morgue, you are gathered to identify the dead, and it appalls the senses, for here they lie as they fell, their eyes unclosed, their forms stiff in the positions in which they died, their gory wounds through which noble lives ebbed away, augmenting and fixing upon the mind the ruthless, cruel and ghastly spectacle. But I will not dwell upon these shocking details.

The place designated by Gen. Rousseau to take my brigade, to refresh them with coffee (which is mentioned in my report) was not far from the headquarters of Gen. Rosecrans, which fact I accidentally discovered by wandering into the room where he and his staff officers were assembled. They were seated on chairs or reclining on the floor, nodding their drowsy heads. The yellow light of a tallow "dip" dimly outlined the cheerless and somber group. The General looked worn and anxious. His disasters on the right were enough to sadden a colder heart than his. I did not speak to him, but I yearned to do so. From my heart welled up a flood of sympathy and devotion to him. I longed to assure him that the Army of the Cumberland was not whipped, and that the men were yet determined and confident. As day began to dawn, he, with his staff, rode to the front, and approaching a line of troops in the rear of the position my brigade had so gallantly won and maintained during the night, he stopped, and with surprise sent for the commander and asked him, "Have you been here all night?" "Yes sir," replied the officer. Then followed words of praise and a telegram from the field to Washington for the officer's promotion. The officer doubtless merited his star and I never envied him, but many an old soldier knows that I drank wormwood and gall when the incident was related to me. "It was fun for the boys, but death to the frogs."

The position assigned to my command early on the morning of the second day was well chosen and an important one to hold. After the batteries were in position and my troops settled in their places, and such defenses constructed as our limited knowledge of engineering made available, my confidence was increased. My hopefulness of triumph in this battle had never deserted me. Having passed through "The Valley of the Shadow of Death" in the cedars, I felt that I would not be killed, and had reached such exaltation of mind as not to care if I was. A new creation, an enlargement of my faculties seemed to pervade me like inspiration! So certain did I feel of myself, that had the command of the army devolved upon me, I could have assumed it without misgivings, and without hesitation have taken the responsibility of directing the battle. I knew no hunger, no thirst, and did not think of sleep. I was never before nor since in such a state of mind, and mention it merely for its psychological interest.

On the afternoon of the third day's fight, from an advantageous position, I made the discovery of a movement of the enemy through a cotton-field in the rear of the brick house on the Nashville and Murfreesboro pike. They were moving toward the ford of Stone river, near the clump of trees which Bragg designated as "Round Forest," which obscured the battery which annoyed us so much. Having called to my assistance Lieut. Martin, of my staff, we continued to watch them, and by counting the mounted officers passing a certain point, estimated their number. Thereupon I directed Lieut. Martin to report to Gen. Rosecrans that a brigade of the enemy were moving to their right — his left. I continued to observe the enemy, and when Lieut. Martin returned, he was despatched again with a message that another brigade, in addition to the one previously reported, was passing to their right (our left). When Lieut. Martin came back to me from the delivery of these messages, he was asked what Gen. Rosecrans said, and in reply he quoted the General's words: "Do you hear that, Crittenden?" and said that Crittenden mounted a horse and dashed off, while Rosecrans' staff officers were dispatched with orders to Negley and others. Soon after this the noise of battle was renewed; the enemy made a furious onset upon Crittenden, and the division of Van Cleve was overpowered by the vigor and number of their assailants, whom they were unable to resist, were driven from their position and forced into the river to make their escape; but reinforcements were at hand, and not a moment too soon. Col. J. F. Miller's brigade of Negley's division came to the rescue, and, fording the river, they rushed upon the enemy. Checking the pursuit, they encountered the foe and drove him, and continued to drive him, capturing a battery and regimental flag. Other troops having joined in the pursuit, it was continued until they were ordered to cease. Crittenden's chief of artillery, Capt. Mendenhall, had now formed a line of fifty-eight guns, which made the welkin ring with their resounding thunder, and lit up the waning day with their lurid lightning. They protruded their red tongues from their open mouths far out into the darkness, as if all the Dogs of War had been let loose to set up pandemonium's reign. This was the beginning of the end. The mind of Bragg was now employed with his retreat; the snap and vim of his first day had oozed away. He made one more spasmodic effort on the next day, when he had another pyrotechnical display. Guenther and Loomis with their guns opened upon Round Forest and the battery ambushed there, when that splendid soldier and gentleman, Gen. John Beatty, with his brigade and some other troops, dashed in and through the woods, and we were no longer disturbed from that direction. The next morning the enemy was gone, and after burying the dead, we marched into Murfreesboro.

CHAPTER IV.

LIGHTS AND SHADOWS.

THE division of Gen. Rousseau was encamped near the town on the Salem pike. The weather was very inclement, with rains, freezes and thaws in frequent succession. The constant moving about of such a large body of men so tramped up the mud that it became over shoe tops in many of the streets of the companies. Our communication by rail with Nashville was intercepted, and about as soon as the road and bridges were repaired, they would be again destroyed by the guerrillas. So for a time it was difficult to provide the army with their most pressing wants, and this and the winter prevented aggressive movements being made.

Bragg had halted at Shelbyville, Tenn., sixteen miles distant, and acted as though he intended staying there until we came for him again. Forage for the horses became very scarce; there was no grass upon which to graze them, and corn was all we could expect to obtain. Immense trains of wagons were sent out on the different roads for it, under large escorts, and often with a brigade of troops and a battery. It frequently fell to my lot to go upon these expeditions. Upon two occasions we advanced to within six or eight miles of Shelbyville, Bragg's headquarters, when the brigade would be deployed in line of battle, with a cordon of pickets nearly as close together as skirmishers, to enclose the foraging ground. The battery would be located with a view to its own safety and to the defense of the position. I have often wondered why Bragg permitted these excursions without greater effort to stop them. It would have required but a small force to have greatly embarrassed and delayed the foraging parties. Sometimes these trains would be over two miles in length. How to convoy a long train of wagons in the enemy's country, on such bad roads as there prevailed, with safety and despatch is a question which has perplexed me greatly to answer. If you place your troops in front, center or rear, the enemy hovering about you and informed of your dispositions, will choose other points of attack, and if you deploy your men all along the road, you will not be strong enough at any point to resist an onslaught. At the more difficult points on the road, which the enemy will know all about, the mules may be stampeded and a few wagons overturned, so as to block the way and throw the train into confusion, and your flankers thrown out on each side of the road, will but very imperfectly guard against these mishaps and delays.

During the first year of the war I reflected much on subjects of this nature, and often, before going to bed at night, I have startled myself with the question, "What would you do should the long roll be sounded?" Then all the contingencies of my situation would be considered and inwardly discussed. Proper orders for the surgeon and quartermaster determined upon, provision for the sick in camp, transportation, rations, ammunition, all required attention; and, when on my long and hazardous marches at this time, I would suddenly ask myself, "What would you do if the enemy should attack you from that ridge? What commands would you give? Where would you place the battery and what would you do with your train? Then I would proceed to criticise my arrangements until another situation would be reached which would require a different set of plans to debate. Thus I have passed hour after hour of the days, and at night come into camp with my brain racked with these perplexing subjects. I found means to answer many of these questions by asking myself what I should do were I in the enemy's place. Then imagining myself in his situation, I would reason thus: "Now, if I counteract what I would do if I were in the enemy's place, I will be apt to counteract him." I think these exercises were useful in many ways, as they increased my resources and readiness with expedients to mitigate the confusion and hesitation which attends a surprise, and prepared me with many well-considered and settled courses of action applicable to various probable conditions; but, notwithstanding this, I am still in doubt on the problem of guarding a train, and incline to the opinion that guarding trains is not an exact science.

Some incidents of my last expedition may be

of interest. The train was a large one, something over two hundred wagons. The escort was composed of two brigades of Rousseau's division, the regular brigade, with their battery, under Lieut.-Col. Shepherd, and my own. Our scouts had discovered corn the day before and guides attended me to point out the places. We followed the pike for six or seven miles, and then turned off on a country road on which woods and fields alternated. Near two farm-houses eighty wagons were left to be loaded, and soon after one hundred wagons were directed on a diverging road, and the balance of the wagons went on. We had entered a cedar thicket. The road was narrow, crooked and rocky, and at places the limestone ledges would crop out to the surface and add to the difficulties of the way.

From this jungle we emerged into open fields again and came in view of a comfortable and rather pretentious farm-house, surrounded at intervals with outhouses, some of these being corn cribs, which fact we could discover by the shucks protruding from the spaces between the logs of which the cribs were built. They were about twenty-five feet square and as many feet high, and covered with a temporary roof. This was removed and the wagons drawn up around the crib, and as corn was thrown into them the logs would be thrown down as the height of the corn lowered until the sides of the wagons were reached. As I drew near to the gate in front of the house by which the road passed, a respectable-looking, middle-aged woman came out to us and cordially invited me to make myself at home in her house, and when I declined, she urged it as a favor to her, for she said, "Your men will respect headquarters, and I will be relieved of annoyance and embarrassment." And now I saw the disappointed faces of some of the young bachelor officers of my staff, who had acquired a special interest in the house by the appearance of two very pretty and stylish young ladies, so I relented, and as we entered I told her my errand, which she received with composure and good grace, and apparently accepted the inevitable. She was much astonished when I inquired for her husband, who was farther south, and her nephew, who had lost a leg in the late battle and was then in the neighborhood. And in answer to her question as to how these things became known to me, I replied that we took the papers. Everything now went on swimmingly; the young people seemed to get on well together, and had arranged for a dance that night. They were sure we could not leave before midnight, "that was impossible with all the wagons to load."

But soon a very different phase of things demanded serious consideration. A sudden rain storm came on and it continued to pour down. I became apprehensive lest the rise of the otherwise insignificant streams might obstruct our passage to the pike. Bragg's videttes were at Redrover and could certainly see us. We did not wish to be caught in a trap, so I sent for my brigade quartermaster, Lieut. Ira Bird, who was a cautious, self-possessed officer, to consult with him as to the feasibility of being able to get the wagons in line on the road to the pike before dark. He thought he could do it, as fortunately the rain abated to a misty drizzle. The number of the men detailed to load the wagons was increased and orders sent to those in charge of the other wagons to regulate their movements so that we could act in concert and be ready to join the line at the proper place and time; the wagons here were dispatched for the road in the cedars as fast as they were loaded. These preparations had scarcely been completed, when I heard ear-piercing shrieks from the old lady in the field near one of the cribs, Her head was covered with her apron to shield her from the rain and, swaying her body to and fro, she continued to scream and wail. She was soon joined by her daughters, who added their cries to those of their mother. I hurried out to learn the cause of this grief and, when the old lady could command speech, she commenced to heap upon me all the abuse which the English language could furnish words for. Then came the accusation:

"You have taken all my corn; we will now have to starve! You promised not to take it all; you said you would leave me enough to take me through the winter and until new corn came! Oh, what will become of us! Oh! Oh! Oh!" to which the daughters echoed in chorus.

As soon as I was able to edge in a word, I assured her that she was mistaken, I had not taken all her corn, and pointing to one of the largest cribs I said, "There, that will carry you through the winter." With a wilder scream than ever, she exclaimed, "That's shucks!" I was stunned as by a blow, then surprise and then a sense of shame pervaded me, and humiliated and distressed me beyond expression. I could only say "I did not know it; I thought that it was corn; it looked like the other cribs which contained corn." I was very sorry, and begged her to believe that I did not intend to take all of her corn. But she would not be pacified, much less reconciled. Now, an old man came up to us, who seemed to have some authority. He showed her that she had plenty of corn, the cribs had only been emptied down to the wagon bed, and that there were several feet of corn at the bottom; and this was mostly shelled. He took my part and defended me by saying that no one could tell that the crib was shucks without examining it carefully. The wagons were all about full, but I stopped the men from taking any more and had them cover up the corn left in the cribs. At length we got the women into the house and out of the rain, but a change had come over the spirits of all. I told her that if her people would let our railroad alone, this means of supplying ourselves would not have to be employed, but that we could not allow our horses to starve. I was glad to get away. They finally shook hands with us, but not very cordially. A soldier has many painful things to do, and is sometimes forced to choose between evils, but duties like this are especially disagreeable, and are opposed to the spirit of chivalry and violate every manly sentiment. But such is war. As Sherman said to Wade Hampton. " You can't refine war. It means bloodshed, widows, orphans, want, waste and destruction." Awful responsibilities rest upon those by whom these evils come.

Darkness was now upon us, and before we were well into the crooked and narrow road in the cedars, many of the Waldron's ridge experiences had to be endured. But this time I did not wait for the stalled teams. After exhausting my patience with waiting for the rear wagons to move, I pressed forward with all the haste the difficulties of the way would allow, and at length reached the place where we had left eighty wagons. Not far from the house on the road was a worrying state of things. Where in the morning there was no water, there was now a pond which seemed to have no bottom. The teams had so worked it up that it was quicksand into which the wheels would sink to the axles. Each wagon was manned by as many as could get about it, to assist it through the slough. I went to the house, from the porch of which I could see what was going on by the light of the rail fires which illuminated the scene. I was also sheltered there from the drizzling rain, which alternating from a mist to a pour, continued through the night.

As at the other house, I was invited to occupy the best room, in which blazed a cheerful fire, and I accepted the offer for the same reason that I did the other, with the exception that there were no young ladies here. We spread our blankets on the floor and lay down with our wet feet toward the fire and had comfort, compared with the poor fellows in the liquid mud helping the floundering mules.

But two persons appeared to be living in the house, a woman and a man. The woman had a delicate and refined face, with a resigned saintliness in her expression that was very touching, and her tired, overworked look excited my pity. Her husband was young enough to be in the rebel army, but I suppose he was exempted for physical disability. He was a tall, slabsided. weak-chested specimen, and was addressed as "doctor." He followed his wife about from room to room, grumbling and fretting, but made no effort to assist her do many things which a gentleman will offer to do for a lady. After they went to bed, we could hear him complaining and crying, more like a baby than a man, while she was trying to console and soothe him with all gentleness and sympathy. This was kept up until the night was far spent. At length I lost my temper and vented it upon him. "Why don't you let that poor, tired woman sleep? Instead of comforting her, you are doing all you can to break her down with your whining about like a sick kitten. Now brave up and be a man, and bear your troubles like a man!" This settled him. The next morning the wagons had gotten out of the pond, and had started on toward the pike. Several mules had perished, and we had a wagon filled with corn and no team to draw it. The doctor was told that we would give the corn if he would deliver the empty wagons to the picket line. He was afraid that his horses would be seized. I offered to give him a letter to the officer of the picket. He said this would be told to the Confederates and a party of them would come and burn his house for helping the Yankees. I then ordered him under pains and penalties to return the wagon, as the only way to meet his case. He thought it very hard that we should take his corn when he had just paid the quantity assessed by the Confederates. I told him that we had come for our share.

We now had a good road to travel, and a heavy load of care and responsibility was lifted from my mind; but the weather grew cold, and turned the rain to sleet, which covered the men like coats of mail and fringed their garments with icicles, but without further mishap we reached our camp. Thus the months of January and February passed away. It was a disagreeable and dismal time.

But early in March, Rousseau's division was

moved over to the opposite side of the town, where our condition improved as the season advanced.

The raids upon the railroad were now less frequent, and the early spring, with its green leaves and grass, had enlivened the landscape. The men were now relieved from further fatigue duty, but of their own motion, proceeded to beautify their surroundings. The grounds were leveled and rammed solid; boughs of trees were dragged over it to give it a finishing touch; over the streets arches were strung, from the center of which was suspended the letter of each company, all entwined with evergreens. The color front of the whole brigade was one continuous line, with a level plain before it extensive enough for the evolutions of a division. The ardor of the men was dampened for a while when their tents were taken away from them and strips of canvas issued instead, but they soon became reconciled and even pleased with the change, for they could now construct more extensive and elaborate quarters by forming the sides with clapboards, which they made themselves, and covering them with the canvas for a roof. They constructed beds by driving forked sticks in the ground, in the notches of which were placed poles suited to the length of the bed, and across these, clapboards or barrel staves were placed. Over this some of the more luxurious ones laid a mattress made of dry leaves placed between two blankets. The use of straw had been abandoned. An old soldier will not have straw on the floor of his tent, but during the first months of service the clamor for straw was a constant source of annoyance. A slab of wood with the flat side hollowed out and resting upon a tripod driven into the ground became a wash-stand and basin. A hat-rack was improvised by cutting off the limb of a tree so as to leave prongs projecting, this also being driven into the ground, and was very useful to hang their accoutrements upon. A barrel sunk in the ground at one end of every company street, with a lid to cover it was the sink into which all refuse must be thrown, and woe unto him who would so far forget himself as to throw even a piece of bacon rind in the street. A grease-spot on the ground would occasion as much fuss and denunciation as a careful housekeeper would display for a stain upon her parlor carpet.

They did not stop here; their æsthetic tastes carried them farther; temples of worship and club houses were undertaken in various styles of architecture from designs furnished by the disciples of Ruskin among their number. The inexhaustible cedar boughs furnished the sides, roofs and decorations of these edifices. On Sunday many of them would be used for religious services, and on other occasions as assembly rooms, concert halls and theaters. The resources of the men never failed, and the *dramatis personæ* for these entertainments were always on hand. I never saw the men in such good spirits; it took but little to make their happiness overflow. A luckless rabbit, straying into the camp, would arouse the highest excitement; the yell increased as the crowd in pursuit gathered successively in the chase. Premature reports of Grant's victory at Vicksburg would frequently set the whole army in an uproar. They had all drawn new clothes; their arms and trappings fairly shone and they looked like the soldiers they had proven themselves to be.

My own comfort was not neglected in the general cheer. A furnished house, vacated by the owners, was within my lines. The keys were brought and everything turned over to me for safe keeping. Beds, furniture, tableware, cooking utensils, servants, stables, all were included in the accommodations. With such an establishment, the thought of sending for my wife was suggested, and she joined me, bringing with her two of the younger children and a nurse. Other ladies, wives of members of my staff, also came. Lieut.-Col. Griffin had gone home to be married, and the happy pair were invited to make their bridal trip to us, so we were a merry party.

My wife had quite an adventure on her way. The railroad at La Vergne was obstructed and the train was attacked by guerrillas; they fired into the car windows, scattering the broken glass about, to the consternation of the passengers who filled the cars. Gen. Brannin was on board and called out, "All lie down on the floor!" My wife, huddling together the two children, crouched down between the seats, and while shielding them as best she could from the falling fragments of broken glass, was asked in an excited voice by her four-year-old boy, "Mamma, will they kill us?" The mother replied, "No, my son; God will take care of us." The lad rejoined : "Then why don't He stop the firing?" But the faith of the mother was not misplaced, for the blue-coats came flying to the rescue and the raiders were driven off before their booty was secured.

Other officers in the different commands had sent for their wives; calls were made and returned, parties given, picnics and excursions to the battle-field were made, and for the first time during the service, something like society was enjoyed. A large oak tree grew near my dining-room, around the trunk of which a spiral stairway had been constructed up to the lower branches, where a platform was arranged to accommodate the band, so music was here added to our many pleasures. The Thirty-eighth started out with the silver band of New Albany, which was composed of practiced artists, but after about six months' service, an order from Washington was received, dismissing all bands, but in some way those of the Seventy-ninth Pennsylvania and Ninety-fourth

Ohio were excepted from this order. So the first division had two bands, and that of the Ninety-fourth Ohio was in my brigade, and I will here express my grateful acknowledgments for the enjoyment they gave us. The Ninety-fourth Ohio could fight and their band could play. Of the many pleasing pictures of these good times which are photographed upon my memory, none are more gladly recalled than the groups assembled about my quarters in the cool of the summer evenings, whiling the too fleeting hours away with music and dancing. Lieut. Hollister, of my staff, was slightly wounded at Stone River, and falling in to the enemy's hands was sent to Libby prison. He had been exchanged and was now with me.

Gen. Willich thus relates an incident of life at Libby prison, which is so characteristic of Hollister, that I will give the gist of it here:

It was the custom in Richmond for parties to visit the prison as groups of persons sometimes do penitentiaries, to gaze upon the criminals there confined. The visitors to Libby were ciceroned by some one of the local clergymen, who would point out such of the prisoners as his frequent visits enabled him to identify, enhancing the interest of the occasion by brief recitals of the crimes and atrocities committed by the persons pointed out. "But," continued the General, "Hollister put a stop to all this, and so covered it with ridicule that it could not be faced. As these groups of sight-seers would commence their rounds, Hollister would stand forth, and turning the crank of an imaginary hand organ in imitation of a showman, who with such gorgeous and seductive language describes the wonders to be seen in the sideshow outside the main tent of the circus, so Hollister, with exhaustless volubility would proceed: "Walk up, walk up, ladies and gentlemen and see the spotted hyena that feeds on dead men's bones. Here is your anaconda and boa constrictor that can swallow a live pig! Walk up, etc," and thus he would continue filling up the intervals with a pretense of grinding an organ at his side. The burlesque and satire which ran through the whole performance was too much for their curiosity, and more abashed than pleased, the visitors would slink away. I have always suspected Hollister of being the principal mover in a trick that turned out to my discomfiture about this time. My landlady, with her daughter, frequently called upon me, ostensibly to get articles they from time to time found they needed, but I think they also wished to see how their belongings were being taken care of. They were not young, fair or agreeable, but I was attentive, polite, and always invited them to meals and waited upon them with all the courtesy I could command. One of these visits happened on the first day of April. Dinner was announced, and they were invited as usual; everything passed off well, until the dessert was reached. The guests were, of course, served first and they proceeded at once to eat, but when the other ladies tasted theirs, a tumult arose that they were unable to repress. Salt had been used instead of sugar! Being the host, with strangers for guests, I was displeased and was profuse with apologies, and begged that the breach of propriety and good manners would be overlooked, as it was not meant for them, but was an April Fool's day lark intended for the other ladies. They, however, had taken no offense, or else their self-possession and culture exceeded my opinion of them, for the old lady calmly replied, "We thought that's the way you'ns made pies."

But we were not wholly given up to festivities, even during these halcyon times. Drills, parades, guard mountings daily reminded us of our duties as soldiers. The system of grand guard at Murfreesboro was the most elaborate and thorough I have ever seen. It was planned and supervised by Col. Von Schroeder, of Gen. Thomas' staff, and so perfect was it with its details, reserves and formalities, that a surprise was impossible. Brigade commanders were in turn detailed as officers in charge, and with their retinue, were expected to make grand rounds. This involved a ride of sixteen miles.

Gen. Rousseau invited a party of his friends to visit him, among whom was the gifted George D. Prentice. Upon this occasion the division was paraded with all the pomp and circumstance of war.

One day the First Brigade was sent out upon the road to Hoover's Gap, to demonstrate upon the enemy, in order to further some designs of the commanding general. We drove in the pickets of the enemy, and advanced several miles upon the road, and bivouacked for the night. The rebels showed fight, and quite an artillery duel was kept up for several hours after dark. The camp was surrounded by a cordon of sentinels, for our isolated position and proximity to Bragg's headquarters admonished us to watchfulness.

After quiet was restored and dispositions for our security made, I lay down to rest, but before daylight, was awakened by Lieut. Sam Vance, the officer of the guard, with the startling announcement, that one of the sentinels was missing. "The relief guard was unable to find him; he had therefore been captured or he had deserted." The countersign was changed, and a picked man was placed upon the vacant beat. It was not long, however, before the suspicions of the new sentinel were aroused — the crackling of dry branches, the rustling of bushes indicated an intention to surprise and capture him also; and thus, with strained nerves, ever on the alert, with gun cocked to fire upon the instant, he spent the night. But when the morning sun dispelled the shadows in the bushes, it also revealed the wide-awake visage of the missing sentinel, who had wandered off his beat in the darkness, and was therefore not found by the relief. The two men had thus for hours been watching and listening to every noise inadvertently made by each, ready upon the instant to fire upon one another at the slightest excuse or provocation. I doubt much, whether any event of the war made a deeper impression upon these two sentinels than the vigils of this night; and they tell the story at their reunion, with all its harrowing details and with blood-curdling effects.

In compliance with my instructions, we returned to camp the next day, greatly to the relief of the ladies, at brigade headquarters. They had been brought so near to the serious business of war, that they could more fully comprehend the responsibilities and dangers involved in it.

When I assumed command of the brigade, many of Col. Harris' staff were retained, but his acting assistant adjutant-general, St. George Vandergrift, was so injured at the bombardment of

Battle Creek, that he was forced to resign, and the good cause lost a useful officer. I filled his place with the adjutant of the Thirty-eighth Indiana, Geo. H. Devol, who, until the close of his service, performed his duties with marked ability. Lieut. J. V. Kelso, quartermaster of the Thirty-eighth, was assigned to me as assistant commissary of subsistence. He afterward, on a day of battle, offered his services as an aid, and did good service in the field. Dr. B. F. Miller, surgeon of the Second Ohio, as brigade surgeon, was another able officer added to my staff. Capt. De Bruin, assistant provost martial, with forty men, was also attached to my headquarters; so with the mounted orderlies and clerks in the various offices, the belonging of brigade headquarters, formed quite a colony.

The designations of commands were again changed, and were now in conformity with the Army of the Potomac. The Fourteenth Corps was under Gen. Thomas; Twentieth Corps under Gen. McCook; Twenty-first Corps under Gen. Crittenden and the Reserve Corps under Gen. Grainger. The ranking corps was the Fourteenth; the ranking division, the First, under

Gen. Rousseau. So the position of the First Brigade was on the right of the Army of the Cumberland. My commission did not give me this precedence, for there were brigade commanders in other divisions who outranked me, but I was the senior officer in the first division. It was during these months at Murfreesboro that I began to know and love that matchless soldier, Gen. George H. Thomas. At that time there was no book in English which applied the orders of battle and grand tactics of the European schools to our third volume. To this subject I devoted much time and study and had instituted a series of drills with my whole brigade, including the battery. The First Michigan Battery had been assigned to me; its former commander, Col. Loomis, had been promoted and was chief of artillery at division headquarters, and the battery was ably commanded by Lieut. Van Pelt. The guns were ten-pound parrots. This battery made a reputation during the war, to use an expression made officially by Gen. Thomas, of my brigade, "that was second to none in this army." At these drills the caissons would be removed to prevent damage to the ammunition; written or verbal orders would be sent by staff officers designating the contemplated movement, and the signal for the word of execution given by raising the point of my sword, when the five regiments in two lines with or without a reserve, would change their front and throw out their skirmishers in conformity with their movements. The location of the battery, the recall of a former line of skirmishers, were all included in the simple words of command designating the order of battle, and given before the change commenced.

It becomes, therefore, very apparent that a command thus educated, would be saved much delay and much of the confusion that attends a change of front while a battle rages.

The First Brigade realized at Chickamauga the advantage gained by this practice. During these exercises I was disturbed by the variations in this drill, which obtained in other commands, and I sought an interview with Gen. Thomas for his decision and orders upon the subject. I represented to him that this might not be the only war that the government might have to engage in, and that it was important that the experience gained in this one should be rendered available in the future, should it ever become the duty of some of us to do battle for our country again. I added that some of us might travel abroad, or meet officers in foreign service, when military questions might be discussed, and then it would be important to designate formations by the generally received terms, in order to be understood. If we did not wish to use an order of battle, let it be omitted, but I insisted that those we did use should be called by their proper names. The General seemed gratified that an interest should be taken in the subject by his officers, and inquired when my exercises came off. I replied, "Every afternoon at four o'clock." He rejoined, "I will be there." He came, and continued to come day after day with a punctuality that was so much observed that crowds of spectators were drawn to our drill grounds.

His presence came to be such a matter of course that any suspected tardiness would be commented on by the men, and threats playfully made among themselves to put him on extra duty for failure to appear on time. In this way I was thrown frequently with Gen. Thomas. I would sometimes during the drill ask him for orders and suggestions, and after the brigade was dismissed he would often ride home with me, and in this way he became known to my household. He, having no children of his own, took much notice and seeming interest in mine, and would take them in his arms and caress them in a manner that won their mother's heart, and made her his friend for life. One day he took the little boy on his knee and, toying with one of his curls, asked him:

"What do you wear this for?" The child rejoined, touching the General's shoulder-strap, "What do you wear this for?" The General, with a smile, replied that the child's question was more difficult to answer than his own.

Another time, in reply to something that was said, the General remarked: "That is like the artist who represented, with three strokes of his pencil, a soldier with his musket on his shoulder, followed by his dog, entering a door." We had not seen the sketch, and he said: "I will show you how it is done," and having made a straight line on a piece of paper, remarked: "That's the side of the doorway;" then joining to this line obliquely a zigzag stroke like a bayonet, said, "and that is the musket," and then lower down on the straight line he attached a short curved one, "and that is the dog's tail—the soldier and the dog are inside." With all his gravity he had a vein of humor in him, and enjoyed a joke hugely.

A story is told of a soldier who applied to him for a furlough and was refused; the soldier pleaded, but the General was obdurate, and at length the man was brusquely asked: "What do you want to go home for?" The soldier replied: "I want to see my wife; I have not seen her for more than a year." The General answered: "Well, I have not seen mine for two years." The soldier, with disgust in his countenance, rejoined: "Humph! me and my wife ain't that kind." This is a true story and is vouched for by that scholar and model gentleman and staff officer, Col. Henry Stone, who served through the war at army headquarters. The Colonel adds that the soldier obtained his furlough.

Gen. Thomas was an undesirable person to approach if you had nothing to say. There was no lounging and twaddle about his office; no slopping of toddies over his desk; if you had no point to make pertinent for his action, he would fix those cold gray eyes of his upon you, and, with his immobile countenance, so embarrass and confuse you that you would wish yourself far away. But, on the contrary, if your matter was within the scope of his appropriate duties, he would give you his undivided attention, and not distract you by continuing to write, or by pretending to write, or by fumbling among the papers on his table (as I have known persons higher in rank than in good breeding do), but would patiently hear what you had to say, and despatch your business then and there, and, should this not be practicable, if you called at the time he said it would be attended to, you would find it done. He was considerate with the humblest private soldier; he was truthful, sincere and even-tempered, and it was traits like these that begot the confidence, respect and love which in so marked a degree were manifested toward him by his men.

One day I caught a glimpse of his inner life. I was complaining to him about something that had gone wrong, and in the heat of my recital, exclaimed: "Any man with a heart would feel as I do!" The General slowly shaking his head, with a sigh replied: "I have taken a great deal of pains in my life to educate myself not to feel." He uttered these words with lengthened pauses between each, as if every one of them recalled some bitter recollection. The elements of character and disposition in both Grant and Thomas had more to do with their success and usefulness than their acquirements, however great these attainments were.

Another way to increase the efficiency of my command received attention at this time. A series of bugle calls was adopted to designate each regiment. By sounding the regimental bugle call from brigade headquarters, then the assembly, and then the officers' call, successively, the same having been repeated by the regimental bugler, I was able to bring the officer in command to me for his orders while his regiment was forming, and thereby be ready to move without delay! This means would be especially useful in directing each organization in battle, when the emergency was pressing, or when it was desirable that my intentions should not be known to the enemy. Many embarrassments followed from the enemy using the same signals and bugle calls as we did. The skirmishers on each side knew when the other was ordered to halt, advance, commence or cease firing. Gen. Sherman knew as soon as Johnston did when Gen. Polk was killed at Pine mountain, our signal officers having taken it from the flags of the enemy. Each army could frequently hear the commands given the other. Gen. Starkweather had a powerful voice, which could be heard at a great distance. The rebel soldiers used to imitate him and repeat his commands to each other, and seemed to find great amusement in it. My voice was weak and low in pitch, and doubtless my officers have been perplexed by its indistinctness. This defect afforded Col. McMynn an opportunity to get off one of his jokes. The Colonel was a ripe scholar and gallant soldier in battle, and ever my devoted friend. But he utterly despised the routine of a soldier's life, especially the drills and parades. He did what was required of him because it was his duty, but not from any pleasure or interest he took in it. One day on drill

Col. Moore failed to hear my command, and dashed up to McMynn and inquired: "Did you hear anything?" The Colonel drawled out: "Y-e-s, I heard that Vicksburg was taken."

There was not time to perfect this system of bugle calls, but Col. Griffin took hold of it with great interest, and his regiment, by much practice, acquired proficiency in it, and the call of the Thirty-eighth Indiana was familiar to the troops in the neighboring camps. There was nothing new in these devices. The Scottish chieftains gathered together their clans with blasts from their bugles, and the movements of the Roman cohorts and legions were regulated by their fifes and trumpets.

CHAPTER V.

THE TULLAHOMA CAMPAIGN.

BUT these happy days came to an end. The invited guests returned home, and another movement upon Bragg commenced.

Much criticism has been expended upon Rosecrans for his delay in assuming the aggressive. The effect of this delay upon Grant's operations at Vicksburg, or whether Bragg sent reinforcements to Johnston or Pemberton, are subjects upon which I have no information. But I think there is another side to the question concerning the propriety of Rosecrans' course. Had a battle been forced upon Bragg, and he been defeated, the vanquished could have made their way to Vicksburg, and, had Bragg been victorious, he could have spared reinforcements for that purpose, and hence Rosecrans, by holding himself before Bragg in a threatening manner, tended to restrain him from weakening his force. But, however this may have been, the offensive now began.

As I understood the plan, McCook and Thomas were to demonstrate at Liberty and Hoover's Gap, while Crittenden swung around to Wartrace to cut Bragg off from his railroad. But the feint upon Liberty was so vigorously and successfully made by Gen. Miller, that Bragg became alarmed, and fell back before Crittenden arrived at Wartrace. Since the war, in an interview with Gen. Miller, he remarked: " Nothing was said to me about demonstrating; I was told to take the gap, and I took it." The General lost an eye in the fight, and for many years carried a bullet in the socket of it.

Our attack at Hoover's Gap at times assumed the proportions of a battle. Col. Wilder met with stubborn resistance, and only carried his point with heavy loss. It would rain and shine during the day, and, in one of the intervals of shine, our line advanced over a newly-mown field, under a brisk fire from the enemy, in the edge of the woods beyond. They had a light battery which did some damage, but the rebels fell back, and we continued to quietly advance.

A farm-house was situated near the right of my line. The household were seated at table for dinner, having waited, I suppose, for the firing to cease, and all was quiet before they began their meal. As the line silently approached the house, files were broken from the right and left to avoid the obstacle, but some of the files marched through the open door of the dining-room, and, as they passed the well-provided table, would help themselves to green corn, new potatoes, fried chicken and other delicacies. The family were all adults, but, dazed and speechless with astonishment and alarm, they remained rooted to their chairs in a helpless stupor and saw their dinner flit away. If the person who described this scene to me could paint it, he would combine in a picture the sublime and ridiculous, the grave and the gay, which sometimes obtain in a soldier's life.

Bragg retreated upon Tullahoma, and Rosecrans followed close upon him, pursuing the same plan of striking at his railroad; but it continued to rain, and rained every day from the middle of June to the 1st of July; the country was covered with water, and in deploying our lines the men had to wade. Crittenden could not reach Bragg's flank in time with such obstacles to be overcome. When his battery would ascend the opposite bank of the swollen streams the muddy water would pour from the muzzles of his guns. With such a state of things, concert of action was impossible, so Bragg got away from us again, destroying roads and bridges as he went. Thus one of the best laid schemes that Rosecrans ever devised was defeated. Like Napoleon, "he was stopped by the elements."

This time Bragg sought refuge in the natural stronghold of Chattanooga, thus establishing the "status quo" of the situation previous to his disastrous invasion of Kentucky. And now plans for a more difficult problem had to be worked out. To comprehend their magnitude, the nature of the country, with its mountains and rivers to cross, must be considered.

The first brigade was sent in advance to occupy Anderson. I did not know at the time for what purpose, for Rosecrans was very reticent about his strategy for the taking of Chattanooga, but I afterward learned it was to protect the pontoons with which we were to cross the Tennessee river. They were hid in the mountains in the neighborhood.

Expecting to remain here for some weeks, we proceeded to make ourselves comfortable, and the camp at Murfreesboro was reproduced, so far as the nature of the ground would admit. Anderson station is situated in Crow Creek valley, which is a narrow strip of fertile land, lying between the mountains. Mr. Anderson, for whom the place was named, owned some seventy thousand acres of land in the valley, the best of which he cultivated himself, and the more sterile portions were rented to what was called "poor white trash." He had forty such tenants, and they were a miserable ignorant lot, there being full-grown men among them who could not distinguish a one-dollar bill from one of two dollars. As these poor wretches wandered about my camp, they were heard to exclaim: "Why, youuns beat all! Weuns have been here forty years an' youuns are fixed better than weuns." They lived, with their large families, in huts with but one room, with a dirt floor, a crazy loom which would occupy one end of the room, and had fewer appliances for comfort than the soldiers had acquired in a few days of their presence among them.

Mr. Anderson was a good old soul, large, fat and jolly. He was also hospitable and at heart kind and liberal. He insisted that I should occupy rooms in his spacious mansion but this I declined, as was my custom, and only departed from in cases where the house was unoccupied, for I had learned very early in war that favors were expected to be reciprocated, and by accepting hospitalities I would be constantly embarrassed by the favors which would be expected and demanded of me in return. The secessionists understood all about such matters and acted upon their knowledge with consummate skill. They would meet you upon the roads as you approached your contemplated camp and, with much suavity, offer their houses for headquarters. They would cover you with compliments, expressing their pleasure in entertaining you, of whom they had heard so much. Riding along together, they would entertain you with the gossip of the neighborhood. "This is Brown's.

I feel sorry for Brown; his sons would join the Confederate army in spite of all their father and mother could do to prevent them — it was of no avail. This place belongs to a man named Jones. He pretends to be an Union man, but he got into trouble in settling an estate of which he was executor. He is not considered reliable." This would be continued until the camp was reached, and then you would find that your mind had been prejudiced against every Union man living about you and that every rebel had been correspondingly whitewashed. Consequently, the Union men, seeing you so intimate with their enemies, would shy off from you, and for a time at least, you would see through rebel glasses.

The family of Mr. Anderson consisted of his wife and two daughters. One of the daughters was married and lived in the neighborhood, and the other was a young lady, who was hurried off to Chattanooga upon the approach of my command. She had heard so much about the Yankees as wild beasts, with "Booty and Beauty" for their motto, that she was afraid to stay at home where such monsters were! This the old gentleman would dilate upon as we became better acquainted.

During pleasant evenings the band would play, while the officers would gather about. Sometimes a regular programme of exercises would be adopted for the entertainment of the visitors. We had a quartette of falsetto voices that I have never heard excelled; negro minstrels, acrobats, jigs and dances gave variety to the amusements. The guests were delighted and astonished at the versatility of my men. Mr. Anderson was completely captivated. I had many young, bright and handsome officers, whom I had introduced to him, and their style and winning manner added to his interest and pleasure. He would whisper his impressions into my ear, and added: "How I wish my Mary was here! How she would enjoy this!" It was evident that she was the light of her father's eyes, and he saw everything as it would impress her. He often referred to Polk's corps, which had once encamped upon his place, and compared my troops with them. He thought my men superior in conduct, appearance and intelligence to Polk's. "I had no idea the Yankees were like you'ns!"

The son-in-law was a "rara avis" and was as good a Union man as could have lived in that locality. He was quite a wag, and full of wit and humor. He delighted to take off the "Governor," as he expressed it, and related many stories of him with more levity than reverence. He had a way, in undertone, of paraphrasing the old gentleman's sentences, and thereby changing the point of his stories, which was very amusing. One time he remarked: "I have won a bet from the 'Governor' by you'ns coming here." I inquired how it was.

"Well, one day as we were returning from the station, where we went every time a train came in, to hear the news of Confederate victories, the 'Governor' was overjoyed with the news and rubbed his hands in great glee as we walked home. At length I stopped and said, 'I will bet you a basket of champagne that before the year is out the Yankees will be swarming over your place thicker than blackbirds.' The old man took me up quick, and thought I was crazy; but it is not a year yet, and here you are!"

He continued: "When you all banished Vallandingham south through your lines, we all turned out in his honor at every place the train stopped, and when he came here I joined in the ovation, during which I heard him exclaim in an excited voice: "You must hold out at Vicksburg! Everything depends upon your holding out at Vicksburg!"

A Confederate general afterward took some offense at Vallandingham's brusqueness and turned away from him, saying for those near to hear: "It is of no use to try; you cannot make a gentleman out of a Yankee." He continued: "I was drafted into the Confederate army once. I let on as if I intended to go. I knew the old man would not let me go, for he is illiterate and I write his letters and keep his accounts, but I was not going to pay out three thousand dollars to get off, so I gave it out that I was going. But the 'governor' forked over the money and I staid at home."

When orders were received to march, I sent for Mr. Anderson and told him that I expected to move my camp soon; and, therefore, if he had any charges against us, to present his claim to my quartermaster and commissary for adjustment, in order that his vouchers might be signed before we left. I continued: "Do this at once, for I do not like to be followed about from camp to camp to sign vouchers." So his accounts were settled to his satisfaction and we parted friendly. I do not know whether or not the old gentleman had noticed the fine print on the vouchers, which read: "To be paid for hereafter, upon proof of loyalty." If he did, I don't think he was sufficiently disturbed by it.

It is interesting to look back upon these times and mark the changes in the Union army which had been brought about by the logic of events. At first we were careful not to "fire the Southern heart" and were fearful of giving offense; we were subservient, meek and even ready to send guards to protect their property. We wished to convince them that slavery cut no figure in the war and that the preservation of the Union was the cause we had espoused. Had it been told my men in the beginning that colored soldiers would be employed, that slaves would be taken as contraband of war, or that their freedom would be proclaimed, there would have been but few, who would have enlisted at that time. But as the war progressed, we found the necessity of the changes in policy. One of my officers, who was extremely sensitive upon this question, thus addressed me: "I have been up to that house on the road. I found the cotton press in operation; the slaves are busy with the crops; the men are all away in the Confederate army; the women are at home in charge of the place, and seem to manage affairs without the men as well as with them, while we have our producers in the ranks, and thus we burn the candle at both ends. We will never conquer the Rebellion in this way. I have now made up my mind that Gen. Butler's contraband order is right."

The influence of the women of the South upon public opinion was paramount. I think they were better educated than the men of the same class. The men had their horses, hounds and various sports, not to mention horse-racing and gambling, which were not so congenial to the women. The men went to college and studied professions in a slipshod sort of way, not so much from any necessity or a desire to excel, as merely to have an ostensible calling, while the women had no such diversions, and were therefore forced to interest themselves more or less with their lessons and books. This, with their great beauty, grace and charming manners, enabled them to lead public sentiment, which they did with much zeal for the cause of rebellion. They sometimes manifested a corresponding hatred for the soldiers of the Union in offensive ways. On the sidewalks of Nashville, after its fall, when about to meet a Union soldier, they would shy off to the wall and clutch away their skirts to prevent contamination, and as the soldier proceeded in his walk, the shutters in advance of him would be successively closed with a bang as he passed.

"When she was good, she was very good,
But when she was bad, she was horrid."

Men are sensitive about the way they impress the opposite sex. The humblest coal-heaver or stevedore, when made conscious that he is an object of disgust to a lady, is hurt away down in his inner consciousness, more than the beautiful offender ever thinks of. The bitterness of the Southern woman will be the last to yield. Men are more forgiving, will sooner forget past strife and will sooner affiliate socially and in their business contact, but the women will cling longer to their prejudices. But the burden of the war bore heavy upon them and they have ever had my sympathy and pity.

There was another class in the South that awakened a stronger and more sincere regard. The Union men of the South had hardships to bear exceeding all others. They were hunted like wild animals by the conscript officers, having to seek refuge in the mountains, in caves and trees, and were only kept from starving by the efforts of their wives and children, who would, by signs and signals, find their hiding places and bring them food. These little children have been whipped by the parties who sought their fathers, to make them tell where they could be found. I saw no sadder sight than a group of these poor fellows, who, emboldened by our presence, had emerged from their places of concealment and stood by the roadside wistfully gazing at us pass. At Sweeden's Cove they timidly asked to see the flag, and when it was unfurled to the breeze, they shouted and cheered it with tears of joy streaming from their eyes. When I told them to seek their holes again, for we were just passing through to another place, their countenances fell and they sorrowfully moved away.

The condition of the Union men of Nashville before it was occupied by our forces has been described to me by one of them. They were looked down upon with suspicion; were forced into the background and deprived of all social or public recognition. But they consoled themselves by the faith that the old flag would come there some day, and that that day would be theirs. I once referred to this when in the company of President Lincoln. In concluding what he had to say about it, he gave one of his characteristic lessons in philosophy:

"The human heart is just the same now as it ever was. Did you ever reflect that Abraham, Isaac and Jacob had the same joy at the birth of a child and the same grief at its death that we have; that when Isaac courted Rebecca, he felt the same trepidation that a young fellow now has when he approaches his sweetheart?

Time and civilization may have modified, but the heart of man is the same."

I do not refer to these actions of the enemy from a vindictive spirit, but their hardships at our hands are so dwelt upon, and reflection so often cast upon the behavior of our soldiers, when they did the same thing to us. Look at the raids made in Indiana and Ohio, and the contributions levied upon Corydon, Salem and other places; the mills that were burned and other private property destroyed without the excuse of necessity, or as the exercise of this means to weaken the strength of an enemy! But cruelties were doubtless committed by both sides, for human nature is just the same, and I only refer to these atrocities to show that they were not committed alone by us, but that they pertain to war, and are sure to follow in its train. I would that those who control events could be impressed with this, to the end that in the future we may have no more war.

Although war is a great evil, it is not an unmixed evil. There are wrongs harder to bear than those of war. Many of the blessings we inherit from our ancestors were achieved by bloodshed. Civil and religious liberty, the rights of man, and his equality before the law, were all wrenched by violence from the grasp of despots and tyrants.

To more fully appreciate the grand results of this conflict, which include the Union preserved and slavery abolished, we have only to contrast the consequences that would have followed the success of the Rebellion. The wranglings over fugitive slaves; the irritations from custom-houses and revenue officers extended along the border; the secession of other states, that would doubtless have further divided us, and perhaps as a climax of disasters, foreign alliances would have been made. Thoughtful minds, both north and south, need not dwell long upon such pictures to enable them to realize that the results of the war are worth all they cost.

Instead of a dismembered country, the jest and sport of foreign nations, we are a great homogeneous power, and command the respect of every civilized nation on the earth.

Col. Damas, speaking of his encounter with Claude Melnotte, says: "I am astonished how much I like a man after I have fought with him."

A sentiment akin to this, I think, obtains with the men who were in both armies, and since the struggle they understand and respect each other more than ever before.

Besides, a military life influences and develops the character of men. It awakens and broadens their minds, and enlarges their experiences. The effect of restraint and discipline upon them was good. Very many, before the war, were devoid of reverence or respect for anything; to them liberty meant license. These were induced to look up to, and defer to authority. Many were taught cleanliness, decorum, self-denial and punctuality, which added to other qualities thus acquired, have made them as useful and successful citizens, as they had been brave and victorious soldiers.

CHAPTER VI.

CHICKAMAUGA'S BLOODY FIELD.

THE road through Anderson, previous to my departure, had become quite a thoroughfare. The Fourteenth Corps moved upon this route for the pontoon bridge over the Tennessee river near Stevenson; consequently I met many of my friends as they passed along. My quarters assumed the appearance of an Inn, where entertainment for man and beast was to be had, and I was glad to have the means and opportunity to offer hospitality to my comrades.

I will not enlarge upon the brilliant strategy with which Rosecrans out-generaled Bragg from Chattanooga. He threatened him in front, while our left and right moved for his rear. Bragg, fearing for his line of supplies, evacuated the city. Rosecrans pursued, but had to divide his forces for this purpose. Crittenden advanced toward Ringgold, McCook descended Lookout Mountain at Alpine, while Thomas debouched at Stevens' Gap. The second division was in advance and confronted the enemy at Dug Gap of Pigeon Ridge, which is a spur of Lookout Mountain. Gen. Rosseau was absent, and the first division was commanded by Gen. A. Baird. Our difficult and fatiguing march over sandy Lookout Mountain was but the repetition of our past experiences crossing mountains.

During the night of the 10th of September the First and Third Brigades of our division got down, and early the next morning we hastened to the relief of Negley, who was in great peril. We now knew that Bragg had been reinforced, and that his troops were massed at Lafayette, south of Dug Gap, and that he was not running away from us, but that he had now assumed the aggressive. Negley's lines having been relieved, he fell back. A brisk fire was now kept up all along the line, the enemy pressing us with much spirit and vigor.

My hay fever was now upon me again, to my great discomfort. I wore dark goggles to protect my eyes, as the glare of the light without them was unendurable. My horse disturbed a hornet's nest in front of my line and became unmanageable, and so slashed me about in the underbrush that my glasses were lost. Overwhelmed with a disaster which would have completely disabled me, I called to my men with much earnestness to find them for me, which they soon did, to my great relief. The men tell this incident with decided relish, that I "stopped the fight to find my spectacles."

Negley formed a new line in the rear, through which we passed, and in turn formed one for him, and thus alternating, we got back that night to Stevens' Gap. The enemy crowded upon us for a time with earnest persistence. It was a narrow escape, and we only avoided capture by stubborn resistance and the skillful management of our officers.

The next day Gen. Baird called on me and rallied me upon my forlorn appearance: "You say nothing is the matter with you, but look like Patience on a monument!" I replied that I was disgusted with the enemy for letting us out of that trap last night. He has lost his enterprise and snap.

The General agreed with me, and added that it was not for us to complain. The fact is that Rosecrans was in a very serious predicament. It was reasonable for him to suppose that Bragg would not have yielded so important a position as Chattanooga, if he could have held it. Therefore Rosecrans very logically took means to pursue, overtake, circumvent and destroy him. To do this in such a country, with such obstacles to overcome, such mountain ridges, roads and streams to pass, all involved the necessity of dividing his forces to accomplish the purpose and cut Bragg off from his line of retreat. Therefore, when Bragg had received large reinforcements from Mississippi, Georgia and Virginia, he had it in his power to concentrate upon Rosecrans and crush him in detail. There were at this time no military operations either East or West to prevent help from being spared to Bragg. On the 11th of September it was well known that Bragg intended to fight. Our right and left were forty miles apart and each of our corps was nearer the main body of the enemy than they were to each other, and not until the 18th of September did McCook succeed in joining

Thomas at Stevens' Gap. Bragg's possibilities during these seven days are fearful to contemplate! To show the straits to which Rosecrans was reduced; he was forced to march his men all night of the 18th to even partially connect his lines for the battle the next day. Our division thus marched all night. The route was defined by rail fires, built also to deceive the enemy. At daylight we halted to make some coffee, and while resting here, Gen. Dan McCook, of Granger's reserve corps, rode up to me and inquired for Gen. Thomas. He explained that a brigade of the enemy had crossed the bridge over the Chickamauga and that he had destroyed it so that the brigade could not get back. McCook thought that this brigade of the enemy could be captured by prompt action, and it was to obtain the order that he sought Thomas. He rode away and soon returned, and remarked as he passed that it was all right, that Brannon was coming to do the job.

Accordingly, Brannon, with two brigades, came along and passed to our left and one of the brigades advanced into the woods and soon engaged the enemy. The noise of battle increasing, the other brigade of Brannon's went in, and now the uproar of musketry and artillery made it significant that Bragg had massed a laige force on our left to cut us off from roads leading to Chattanooga, and that the rebel brigade that McCook referred to, was but a small portion of this force. Our division was now ordered to enter the fray on Brannon's right. My brigade was on the right of the division. Where roads forked I left my battery with a regiment to guard it, and moved forward in two lines. We soon met the enemy and pushed upon him and drove him handsomely. I was cautioned about firing to right lest I should fire into our own men. The enemy still yielded to our steady advance. Another staff officer rode up and informed me that we connected with Palmer on the right. I was advancing with our right refused, but we now straightened the line, and, as the ground became more suitable for artillery, my battery was ordered up, and also the regiment left with it. We still continued to press the enemy back, stepping over their dead and wounded and taking prisoners as we progressed. At length we came to a rail fence in front of an open field, which sloped towards us from the woods beyond. Across this field the enemy fled, when a rebel battery emerged from the woods and came toward us and wheeled into position. I called out to Col. Anson G. McCook, of the Second Ohio, "Anson, do you see that?" The Colonel, radiant with delight, replied: "I see it!" and made a dash for the battery, but they did not unlimber, but sped back the way they had come to the shelter of the wood. We were all now very happy. Col. Moore, elated with satisfaction, said to me: "They can't fight us; the 'Bloody First' is too much for them!!!" In this congratulatory state of mind my brigade surgeon approached me with dismay in his face. I addressed him brusquely:

"What is the matter, Dr. Miller?" He replied: "I have been in the hands of the enemy." I rejoined: "What do you mean?" He answered: "I mean to say that the enemy is in your rear and on your right. They have taken my field hospital with all the wounded! They have captured Capt. DeBruin, the provost guard, and all the prisoners and are coming down upon you like a pack of wolves." The shock of these words and their dreadful import can be better imagined than described. Bracing myself up to meet the impending crisis, every staff officer was despatched in a different direction; one to Palmer, one to Baird, one to Thomas, one to Reynolds, to Johnson, and to any one who ought to have the information. I asked for help and directed my staff to say that I would hold my position until reinforcements came, for the division ammunition train was parked near the place I had left the battery, and was in peril. Lieut. Devol proceeded to the right to caution Palmer and came suddenly upon the rebel lines. With much self-possession he concealed his knowledge of their presence, and sidling off, got away and reported to Gen. Thomas the situation, who ordered him to direct any troops he met to my support. I gave the command: "First order of battle, face to the right!" and the enemy on the right opened their fire. The fire from the woods beyond the open field was also renewed, and one of my regiments on that front was held to reply to it. The Ninety-fourth Ohio was not deployed, but held in reserve, they being on the left of the second line. The brigade proceeded to execute the command as if on drill, and as the battery came swinging to its position in the new front, I called out to Van Pelt, that if he could not place the whole battery to place a section. He was confident that he could bring the whole battery to bear. And now the conflict began! Van Pelt fired sixty-four rounds of double shotted canister right into their faces without seemingly disturbing the enemy, and they continued to press me on both fronts, but my men held on with a persistence born of their past experiences and successes. It seemed as though a terrible cyclone was sweeping over the earth, driving everything before it! All things appeared to be rushing by me in horizontal lines, all parallel to each other. The missiles of the enemy whistling and whirring by, seemed to draw the elements into the same lines of motion, sound, light and air uniting in the rush! The uniformity of these lines was ever and anon disturbed by the roar and shrieks of cannon balls and shells, to subside again to the new direction now assumed by nature. Intuitions of passing time were lost and lives were lived and yielded during these brief moments! At length the enemy closed in upon us as if like flame, or a rushing tide, they would lap us up; they were on our right, front and rear, and we had to cut our way out as best we could.

My losses were dreadful to contemplate! Seven hundred and fifty men were *hors de combat*, nearly every horse in the battery was killed; the gallant Van Pelt, with twenty-five men, was cut down at the guns; the enemy got off with one of them, but the others were saved in a disabled condition. Reinforcements came too late for my brave boys. They, too, were struck as by a whirlwind and hurled into disorder. Then Johnson and Reynolds, with their divisions, appeared and were able to hold the field. Gen. Thomas had come up and directed me to re-form some broken lines of troops, which I did, and then passed some rods to the rear, where I found my shattered brigade in column of regiments, calmly awaiting orders as if nothing unusual had happened. We afterward learned that my lines had struck the ford of Chickamauga, near the railroad station, where Bragg's reinforcements from Lee's army were arriving. We therefore, unconsciously, threatened an important point that Bragg could not afford to yield without a desperate effort to defend it, and fortunately for him, he had the forces at hand to do so.

The unfortunate report that I connected with Palmer was brought about by a brigade, which Gen. Palmer had sent on a reconnoissance to find the right of Thomas. They having found it, returned with the required information, but they left the gap open after creating the impression that they had closed it.

Toward evening my command joined Johnson and Reynolds, and we had another battle on the same field we had fought over in the morning. The artillery was prominent in this engagement, and it was after ten o'clock that night before all was quiet.

Anxious to give my men some rest, Gen. Baird was sought for orders, having notified the officer on the right of my intention, and an orderly was left to mark the spot and to communicate with me should necessity arise. I had not proceeded far until the General was met searching for me, so I retraced my steps with him to my command, and not finding it where I had expected, the General became apprehensive that we were lost in the woods and might wander into the enemy's lines. I began, myself, to feel uneasy and called out "Orderly!" "Sir!" was the prompt response of the good soldier, from the spot where he had been placed, but he was alone. He informed me that the brigade had moved back; the officer on the right feared a flank movement of the enemy. The left of our line had been fired on: "But. you told me to stay here, and I staid." Gen. Baird conducted us to a large open field, where my men laid down their weary bodies to rest.

Our movements in the night had so confused me that I did not know even the points of the compass. Lieut. Devol was the only staff officer with me, the others and the orderlies having lost me in the darkness, so I directed the lieutenant to find out our whereabouts; whether that house off yonder was Kelly's, where we halted in the morning before the battle began. He was urged to learn all he could about the events of the day, and to take the two canteens along and fill them with water. I tried to impress him with my locality in order that he might find me when he returned. So I sat down upon the ground, holding the bridle of my horse in my hand to await news and water. But I waited and waited, but did not see him again until morning; he too had lost me! My condition was indeed forlorn and miserable! A cup of coffee that morning was my only nourishment since the evening before at Stevens' Gap; my inflamed eyes itched and burned, asthmatic coughing and breathing, and all the discomforts of hay fever added to my sorry plight. At length pity for my poor horse, who had fared no better, diverted my mind from my own privations to his. A rail fence was found to which he was hitched, but in removing the saddle, my pistols fell from the holsters, and with all my groping about I was unable to find them. Observing a light in the woods at some distance off, I called out and found that it was the bivouac of Simonson's battery. They knew me at Perryville and a party of them hastened to my assistance. They found my pistols, made my fire and spread my blanket before it, and would have shared their supper with me, had I permitted them to rob themselves.

I was soon alone again. It would not do to fall asleep, even had I felt like doing so, for I was anxious about the coming of my staff officer.

More than twenty-three years have passed away since that distressing night; other horrors have since filled my mind, but the long painful vigil of that night of gloomy forebodings is yet fresh in my memory! As I crouched, brooding over my lonely fire, the incidents of the day passed in review before me, renewing each sad scene. I was surprised and shocked again and again at the bleeding bodies of much loved comrades. I mourned again over the prostrate form of Lieut.-Col. Maxwell, of the Second Ohio, whom I assisted to an ambulance after the battle of the morning. He was shot through the lungs, the bullet entering his breast and making its exit at his back. He wore a light buff vest which was soaked with his blood, which made him a ghastly spectacle to look upon. His own father could not have embraced and wept over him more fondly than I did. He was not dead, and ignoring my cause of grief, tried to console me for the reverses of the day, and encourage me with hope of ultimate victory, as if my disasters caused my emotion. He was a favorite officer and I was sincerely attached to him.

A singular fatality seemed to have followed

this brave soldier thoughout his whole career. He was wounded at Perryville, his leg being broken. He recovered to be wounded again in his next battle at Stone river, a bullet passing across his throat. From this precarious wound he had recovered, and he had now, as it was believed, received his death blow. Here let me finish the story of this most unfortunate man. After a long and dreadful struggle for life, he again recovered and was appointed to the colonelcy of one of the new Ohio regiments, and during his first engagement with it he was again wounded, a bullet striking the pommel of his saddle and glancing under him, made a grievous wound, and again he finally recovered. After the war he was appointed assessor of internal revenue. One day a peddler sold him a contrivance to prevent burglars from tampering with locks, by causing the explosion of a percussion cap. While the Colonel was exhibiting it to some friends, a piece of the cap flew into one of his eyes and put it out. The last time I saw him was at a meeting of the Society of the Army of the Cumberland at Dayton, Ohio. He was master of ceremonies and seemed very happy in meeting with his old comrades again. A few weeks afterward the Associated Press despatches announced the death of Gen. O. C. Maxwell. He was found dead in his room with an empty pistol in his hand. The poor fellow had great trouble, and had lost all his money, and when his comrades departed his mind plunged again into his misfortunes and its balance was lost.

At daybreak the next morning, according to orders from Gen. Baird, we took the position so persistently held by us throughout the day. We formed in two deployed lines along a wooded ridge, behind us an open field, and before us the ground sloped away from view in the timber. Our division was on the extreme left of the army and covered the road to Rossville and Chattanooga. The Third Brigade was on my right and the regular brigade on my left. We hastily threw up breastworks of rails and such logs as could be found, in front of each line. The second line, owing to the declivity of the ridge, was very near the first.

These dispositions had scarcely been made, when the enemy commenced a furious assault upon us. I instructed my second line to move to the works of the first and deliver their fire after the first, by my order, should commence to fire, then each was to load his musket shielded by the same shelter, and thus to alternately load and fire while the conflict lasted. The enemy prepared for this attack with much deliberation. Their battle flags (a white ball on a dark field) were planted along their line to form by, and their officers, with swords held across their breasts with both hands, facing their men, dressed their line with commendable coolness and vim. When they got ready, they made a dash upon us. We had reserved our fire while they were making these preparations, but now we gave them a warm reception with an incessant outpour of bullets. The battery of the Third Brigade had a flank range along my front by some of their guns. This range was a narrow open space covered with green, mossy grass. In this space we held the enemy while the battery mowed them down. During this assault, some of the rebels threw away their guns and rushed toward us and jumped over our works for safety. They did not wish to be considered deserters, but they preferred the risks for the short distance to us rather than the longer one of danger going away from us, pursued by the galling fire we were pouring into them.

At length the ardor of the enemy having been cooled, they drew back to reform their lines and screw up their courage for another effort to drive us from our position. This they did again and again, only to be as often repulsed, and they kept this up at intervals all during the day. Toward evening they made another desperate effort. One of Negley's brigades was sent around our left as if to turn the rebel flank, but was driven back in some disorder. Flushed with this success, the enemy pressed their advantage and came down upon our left and rear. Gen. Baird was alive to the critical condition, and ordered our second line to face about to meet this new danger. The enemy now put forth all their force. The battle raged on our front, left and rear. Other disorganized troops prolonged our second line. The enemy seemed to be animated with new life; desperation had seized them; they would sway and surge from one part of the line to another to find a yielding point, but no such point was found. Our men fought as if they felt the awful responsibility laid upon them; they comprehended the vital importance of the position they held and the disasters that would follow the abandonment of it, and with a courage born of necessity, summoned all their powers of resistance to hold it. At length the rebels in our rear slackened their fire, then wavered, and then fled into the woods the way they came, pursued by the cheering, happy victors! I had to restrain my men from continuing this pursuit and leave it to those who had prolonged my second line, for I apprehended that an increased effort would be made upon our front, reinforced perhaps by those just driven from our rear, but their efforts grew feebler, and then quiet seemed to reign.

Ammunition was now growing scarce, and only after diligent search could a few rounds be found. Night was now coming upon us, and I passed down the line and reminded my men of the rebel trick to assault us at nightfall, when it would be too late for us to regain any loss we might sustain. They were cautioned, therefore, to save their ammunition for this emergency.

Having returned to my position, Capt. Forsyth was awaiting me. He informed me that orders were for us to fall back. I could not believe it, and argued the point with him and reminded him that we had whipped the rebels here all day, and pointed to our troops who seemed to be moving to our left. "Do you see that another assault is to be made upon the enemy's right?" Forsyth left me as if I had convinced him of his error. Not long after this a staff officer, from division headquarters, brought me an order to fall back. He had been down the line and had given it to regimental commanders, but they told him that such an order would have to come from me to be obeyed. The men were in high spirits, and confident; the day had been one of victory to them. This order to fall back was the first intimation we had received that any reverses had befallen our right.

I now noticed that the troops before observed in the field in our rear were still passing to the left and rear in greater numbers, and that our troops on the right were drawing off. The fire from the enemy was again renewed on the right, and increased as it approached my front, so my two lines were faced about and in good order they fell back across the field toward the woods over which Granger had fought a fierce battle during the afternoon.

Here we found a discouraging state of things. The ground was strewn with the debris of battle; dismounted cannon, overthrown wagons, and all that disorder which a recent battle-field presents. In whatsoever direction we turned our gaze we beheld our men wandering about singly, or in groups, without purpose, without leaders, disorganized, but not demoralized or panic-stricken. Several times I approached officers of higher rank than I and offered them my command, as a nucleus to form upon for any undertaking they thought best to make. One officer advised me in a confidential, friendly way, to take my men off as best I could, and if I found that I could not take my battery with me, to cut loose the horses and try to save them, if possible. These words and the manner of the officer utterly amazed me. I had not imagined that we could be reduced to such straits. In reply to my question, as to what he meant and what had happened to the army, he told me the sad news that Rosecrans, with McCook and Crittenden, had fallen back to Chattanooga. This was the unwelcome story told me by my old friend, Gen. Dan McCook, who had asked me, the morning before where he could find Gen. Thomas, whom he sought for orders for the capture of a rebel brigade, and who afterwards, at Kenesaw Mountain, with the brave Gen. Harker, gallantly yielded up his life.

I now became convinced that it was my duty to collect these scattered men. It would soon be too dark to do so, and they would lay their tired bodies down in the woods, fall asleep and perhaps be captured by the enemy. I was the ranking officer of the division present, so I assumed command, and ordered all of the First Division, Fourteenth Army Corps, to fall in. The call of the Thirty-eighth was sounded, and when its familiar notes were heard and recognized, many were brought to us. As we slowly proceeded on the road to Rossville, every one was urged to fall into my column. The Second Ohio was in advance, and Capt. Ambrose was ordered to deploy his company and direct every man who was not assisting the wounded, to fall in. We came to a soldier who was bearing on his back a wounded comrade who clasped him about the neck like a little boy riding a bigger one when playing at "horse," and they, too, joined my column and were helped along. Groups waited for us on the roadside, and as the bugle's notes penetrated the woods and hills, men came gathering in from all directions, swelling my column to huge proportions. At length we arrived at Rossville. The first division was ordered ten paces to the front and closed up. Then observing Gen. Crufts, I turned the balance over to him and lay down with the men to rest.

We were soon, however, aroused and ordered to Chattanooga, but on the way this order was countermanded, and we returned to Rossville and took position on the ridges near the town, While moving to our place in the line, and waiting for those in front to move on, I observed a fire in an orchard by the roadside. As the way in front was blockaded, I dismounted and approached the fire, and recognized the familiar face of Capt. Willard, of Gen. Thomas' staff. The Captain offered me a split-bottom chair, the only one about, but I took it and sat down.

Sprawled about on the ground, lay the tired officers of the staff. Willard was the only one awake. I sat there a few moments, taking some comfort from the welcome and the fire, when I felt a gentle pressure upon my shoulder, then a familiar salutation, and then at once rose to greet Gen. Thomas! The question was argued as to who should take the only chair, and neither took it. The weather was discussed, but he made no reference to any battle having been fought, and I did not. Desultory subjects were touched upon, but nothing about this night march and disposition for battle, which was expected before another day should dawn. There was blood upon my cheek where a ball had grazed it; I had been knocked down by the fragment of a shell which struck my shoulder and blackened my breast to the waist; my horse had been shot under me during the day; a few hours before I had seen another of my field officers shot in the head while his eyes were answering mine in the joy of success; I had lost many valuable officers and men, many of whom the General had met at my quarters at Murfreesboro. I expected him to inquire about the fortunes of my command, but he said not a word to indicate that anything unusual was transpiring, and neither did I. I asked for no orders; my division commander would give them to me in time; so after a chat, I bade him good morning and rode away. He had educated himself "not to feel."

The next day we had fortified the position without causing any demonstration from the enemy. We could not have been driven from it by any force they could have brought to bear upon us, but it could easily have been flanked. So that night we fell back to Chattanooga. I was designated to bring off the rear. The staff officer who brought me the order, informed me that there had been some strife for this honor, but that it had been accorded me, as being the last organization to leave the field of battle. I thought that my honors came inopportunely, for I was nearly worn out, having been without sleep during the nights of the 18th, 19th, 20th and 21st, and now I had to put in another night with work. But we proceeded to make the necessary preparation. We thought the troops made a great deal of unnecessary noise in moving off, but this the rear guard always thinks.

We feared the enemy would detect the movement and assault us in a weakened state. I caused trees to be felled to drown the noise and to create the impression that we were still fortifying, but we withdrew, skirmishers and all, without the loss of a man, and at nine o'clock in the morning were in line awaiting the approach of Bragg. Thus we were at Chattanooga, the objective point of the campaign!

CHAPTER VII.

A GREAT BATTLE—IN LENGTH, BREADTH AND THICKNESS.

THERE is nothing that produces upon a man so profound an impression as a great battle; nothing which so stirs and tests the soul within him; which so expands and strains the functions of sensation and so awakens all the possibilities of his nature! There is nothing which so lifts him out of himself; so exalts him to the regions of heroism and self-sacrifice; nothing which so surcharges and permeates his receptive faculties, and so absorbs and employs all the powers of his mind and body as a great battle! Human nature here finds its ultimatum and is undergoing its greatest strain.

I have witnessed the smoking volcano, the glowing meteor and the flashing lightning; have heard the resounding thunder in the heavens; I have been in storms and tempests on land

and sea, but a great battle comprehends them all. In one you are an awe-stricken, helpless spectator, perhaps a victim, but in a great battle, you are an actor and are animated and inspired to perform the part for which the occasion fits you.

While Rosecrans was busily employed in strengthening his position against further attacks, Bragg was as industriously investing us, perhaps preferring to reduce us to terms by starving us than to take the chances of successfully fighting us. Both armies had suffered greatly in the late battle. Rosecrans estimated his aggregate loss at 16,336 men, and from the best sources, Bragg's aggregate loss was 26,264 men, making the sum of both, 42,600 men. This frightful loss indicates that the battle of Chickamauga was one of the most destructive fought during the war. Both armies were stimulated to their utmost capacity. We had always defeated Bragg, and now held Chattanooga, the gateway to northern Georgia, and therefore felt confident and aggressive. On the other hand, Bragg had been strongly reinforced. Longstreet's men would say to those of Bragg: "Stand back and let us show you how we do it!" Thus both armies were put upon their mettle and vied with each other.

I once met Gen. Manny, of the Confederate army, then a member of Congress from the State of Tennessee, and during a conversation about the war, which ensued, I asked him jocosely: "What possessed you to fight us so unnecessarily hard at Chickamauga?" The General replied: "To tell you the truth, I have always thought that you fellows did more than your duty."

The enemy took a strong position on Missionary Ridge, and also on Lookout Mountain and the valley west of it, and thereby commanded the approach to Chattanooga from Bridgeport, by the roads or river near it. Extensive raids were made upon our communications and our bases of supply to the northward, and short rations and short forage began to be felt. All supplies had to be transported over circuitous routes over the mountains on the north side of the river, but with these precarious means of supply, the teams weakened by scant food, became so feeble that they could not haul much in excess of what was required by themselves, and the necessary escort on the way.

To relieve his army from the calamities which now threatened it, Gen. Rosecrans, with his chief engineer, Gen. W. F. Smith, devised a brilliant scheme to shorten the route and obviate passage over the mountains to Bridgeport, our depot of supply. They planned to send troops on floats, with pontoons down the river under cover of night, to Brown's Ferry, a few miles below in Lookout Valley; then to seize the position and throw the pontoons across the river and thus enable reinforcements, which would be sent down on the north side, to cross over on the bridge and hold the place until Hooker's forces could come up and hold the valley.

But Rosecrans was at this time relieved by Gen. Thomas, and these well considered plans were carried out by Gen. Thomas, with the approval of Grant. The Military Division of the Mississippi was created, with Gen. Grant as commander. The Twentieth and Twenty-First Corps were consolidated and designated the Fourth Corps, under Gen. O. O. Howard. The

Eleventh and Twelfth Corps were also consolidated and denominated the Twentieth Corps, under Gen. Jos. Hooker. The reserved corps was assigned to the Fourteenth Corps, which was now commanded by Gen. Jno. M. Palmer; the first division, Fourteenth Corps had Gen. R. W. Johnson for commander. The brigades had also been consolidated. The first now commanded by Gen. W. P. Carlin, was composed of nine regiments, viz: Second, Thirty-third and Ninety-fourth Ohio, Tenth Wisconsin, Fifteenth Kentucky, Thirty-eighth, Forty-second and Eighty-eighth Indiana, and the One Hundred and Fourth Illinois. Col. Hapeman, of the One Hundred and Fourth Illinois, was a painstaking officer, and Col. Humphrey, of the Eighty-eighth Indiana, was a good soldier and an old comrade of mine during the Mexican War.

I felt much like a non-commissioned officer reduced to the ranks, to lose the command I had so long held, but Gen. Carlin was my senior in rank, and such hardships frequently occur in armies. He, with a delicacy which was only excelled by his soldierly qualities, said to me:

"No one can properly manage nine regiments

in a fight. I wish you would still retain charge of your old brigade." So while Gen. Carlin was officially in command of the brigade, I still had a general control of my old command, and not to be excelled in courtesy by this splendid officer, I exercised my authority with a proper deference to his.

While Chattanooga is almost impregnable from an assault from the north, drawing their supplies from the north, it is weak when attacked from the south by a force whose base of supply is in the south. We were encompassed about and commanded by the strong and elevated positions of the enemy, which could be held with an inferior force.

Hooker was now advanced into the Lookout valley and had driven the enemy to the western slope of Lookout Mountain. He made several very gallant and successful fights, the one at Wauhatchie being especially brilliant.

Sherman, with the Army of the Tennessee, had now joined us, and on the 23d of November had succeeded in crossing his army on the pontoons at Brown's Ferry, with the exception of the division of Gen. Osterhaus, of the Fifteenth Corps,

A GREAT BATTLE. 171

which was prevented by the breaking and destruction of the bridge. The river was bank full and rushed by like a torrent. Gen. Osterhaus was assigned to Hooker, and with Cruft's division of the Fourteenth Corps, and Geary's division of the Twentieth Corps, formed Hooker's column which so gallantly attacked Lookout Mountain the next day. Hooker was expected by Grant to demonstrate upon Bragg's left on the mountain from his location in the valley, while Sherman was to pass up the river, shielding his movements from the enemy, and cross the river again on pontoons already provided, and with as much surprise to Bragg as possible, to fall upon his right on Missionary Ridge, and after he had driven Bragg's right, Thomas was to follow up the success of Sherman and continue it all along the ridge from right to left. To facilitate the prompt consummation of these designs, Thomas carried Orchard Knob by storm, and brought his lines into position in front of Missionary Ridge. On the 24th, according to programme, Sherman made a successful crossing of the river and assaulted as intended. But Bragg was much stronger here than either Grant or Sherman expected. The natural defences were augmented by fortifications difficult to surmount. The next day the Fourth Corps was sent to Sherman's assistance, and later in the day he was further reinforced by another division of the Fourteenth Corps, and yet Bragg's right was not turned or driven. While thus awaiting Sherman's movements, Thomas was not seriously engaged on the 24th, and we lay in line upon our arms and were at leisure to observe what was occurring around us. At length reports of artillery were heard in the direction of Lookout valley! At first we were uncertain whether they were from our batteries or those of the enemy, but, by noting the intervals between the reports from the guns and the explosion of the shells, and that both these reports came close together, we reasoned that the shells were coming toward the mountain, and hence they were Hooker's guns that were firing.

Soon the rattle of musketry was heard and Hooker's lines were discovered swinging around the point of the mountain with their right closely hugging the perpendicular palisades and his left stretching down the rugged sides of the mountain. When the men beheld this unexpected sight, and realized that Lookout Mountain was being assailed, they were struck with amazement. The audacity of such a conception, and the hardihood of trying to execute a design so hazardous and impracticable, they were wholly unprepared for! They had gazed upon its rocky slopes and lofty crest which towered on high more than two thousand feet above the level of the sea, and from which seven states could be looked down upon! During the siege they had heard with awe and dread the thunders of the heavy batteries safely planted upon its level summit, protected by the impregnable wall which on three sides frowned upon and defied approach. The sublime majesty of the mountain, standing forth in the sunlight, or obscured as wrapped in the black draperies of a tempest, mysteriously fulminating, all enhanced the grandeur of the surroundings and augmented the moral effect of the position of the enemy.

I once asked Gen. Thomas why Bragg did not use these guns more effectively upon us; that we seemed to be at his mercy. The General replied that the damage done by them had been trifling. He referred to the expense incurred every time one of those guns was fired, and added that "the Southern Confederacy had no money to throw away." But we were much disturbed in mind by these huge shells, which resembled a joint of six-inch stovepipe and suggested danger.

Hooker continued to advance in the face of a steady fire from the enemy, who, being on the defensive, could shelter themselves behind the rocks. But our boys did not seem so much occupied in resisting the enemy as overcoming the difficulties of the way. They loaded and fired as they found occasion; the main business was to climb over and around the rocks and to get over as much ground as possible, and they slowly and steadily advanced, driving the enemy from rock to rock. As they approached the white house on the side of the mountain, the ground became smoother, and the enemy, from their rifle-pits and other defences, made a stand and redoubled their fire. Our line for a moment seemed to hesitate, but the color rank continued to move on and step by step to lengthen their distance in front of the line. This was an anxious moment for the earnest spectators, but when the line braced up and rushed to the colors and drove the enemy again, shouts of joy and admiration burst forth from thousands in the plain below. In my enthusiasm I exclaimed to Gen. Johnston: "Why can not some of us idle fellows go to help them!" And it was not long after this that the First Brigade was ordered to report to Gen. Hooker.

It was, however, late in the afternoon before means to cross the Chattanooga creek could be procured. Misty vapors would at times, like a drawn curtain, hide the combatants from our view, and then only could be heard the uproar of musketry and artillery, and occasionally the explosion of a shell would pierce the lowering haze and light up the scene. We had a battery across the river, on Moccasin Point, which had a range along the mountain side, and which promoted the success of the enterprise.

Gen. Carlin sent me with the advance to find Gen. Hooker, report the command and receive orders. Hooker was expecting us and directed me to relieve Gen. Geary, whose line was in front of the white house. I was informed by Gen.

Hooker that he was nearly out of ammunition, and he added: "But I won't yield an inch of my ground, not an inch!"

It was after dark before the brigade succeeded in ascending the rugged way and the relief of Geary's troops was effected. Osterhaus was on the left of Geary, and reached down the mountain. The lines did not connect. The right of Osterhaus was behind the left of Geary, and therefore there was a considerable space on Geary's left and rear exposed to a flank attack, should the enemy discover the weak place. I was at the white house, while Carlin and Geary were out attending to the adjustment of the lines, when an officer with a major's shoulder-straps burst in upon me and dropping down on the floor limp and fagged tried to speak. It was some moments before he could utter an intelligible word, and when he could catch his breath, he gasped out in spasmodic jerks: "I am not scared — but exhausted with climbing the rocks, to tell you the enemy have found a gap between Geary and Osterhaus, and are moving into it!"

I did not wait to hear more, but rushed out to find Carlin and provide for the emergency. The havoc that might result from an attack at night in the rear by the enemy, who knew the ground much better than we did, was at once comprehended. Three regiments were hastily brought to the spot and a line formed perpendicular to the left of Geary's and right of Osterhaus, and thus the gap was filled, but not a moment too soon, for as each regiment successively came into line, they opportunely confronted the enemy, who was also successively forming his line.

The clatter of musketry as it rolled down the line, soon proclaimed that the gap was filled. A brisk fire was now kept up on both sides until after ten o'clock, and ceased only by the retirement of the enemy. This was the night fight on Lookout Mountain, often referred to, and which attracted so much attention in the plain below during its continuance. The next morning when the sun had dispersed the clouds from the beetled brow of the grand old mountain, and the troops in the valley beheld the starry flag of the Union floating on high, shouts and cheers arose, which taken up from right to left, directed all eyes to the joyful sight, presaging further triumph and honor to the flag we loved!

Hooker proceeded down the mountain by the Summertown road toward Rossville, still to threaten Bragg's left, and to coöperate in the assault on Missionary Ridge, while we returned to Chattanooga by the river road, now a thoroughfare again, and joined our division on the right of the army.

The bridges over the streams which Hooker had to cross had been destroyed, and so delayed him that he could not partake in the direct onslaught upon Missionary Ridge, and therefore the first brigade of the first division, fourteenth army corps, was the only brigade in the army that fought on both Lookout Mountain and Missionary Ridge, a distinguishing honor we are all very proud of.

The enemy had thrown up earthworks a short distance in front of the ridge, and had dug rifle-pits on its side. We debouched from the woods and carried the earthworks, advanced a short way up the ridge with the skirmish line and there were halted. The enemy at the summit and extremity of the ridge extended beyond our right, and had a battery of six-pounders beyond our right. The Union lines extended upon our left for several miles, and the flags and glittering bayonets formed a grand and formidable sight. Situated thus, with our right in air, we did not expect to charge with the main line; of course, we would refuse our right and be assisted by a flank fire of troops on our left after they had reached the summit. The earthworks were occupied on the reverse side by our men. The space between them and the base of the ridge had been the enemy's camp, from which they had just been driven. They had constructed shelters of clapboards loosely laid on sticks, and were made to crawl under for protection from the dew or sun, for they would shield them from nothing else. There was a slight, desultory firing kept up along the line. I had sent our horses to the woods in charge of a slightly wounded soldier, and had sought shelter from the observation of the enemy under one of the sheds, but the coming and going of the regimental staff officers drew attention to me from the rebels, and they directed their fire upon my shed and caused it to rattle as if in a hailstorm. Many of the bullets passed through the thin boards and routed me out of this trap. I sought refuge behind the earthworks with the men, and was followed by a solid shot from the rebel battery, which plunged into the earth in front of me, and had it been an explosive shell, this story would not have been written.

Gen. Carlin now hastily passed by and said that it was reported that the enemy were coming around our right, and ordered me to bring a company and follow him quickly to investigate the matter. The report was found to be untrue, but while we were examining the locality I happened to glance toward our lines and observed them in motion up the ridge. The whole line, as far as the eye could reach, was steadily climbing the hill. When I told Carlin, he exclaimed, with more emotion than he had ever before manifested to me: "My God, who will take the responsibility of this!" We both assumed that the charge had been ordered. Having sent the company back to its regiment, we hastened to the lines, but made no effort to restrain them; it was now too late for that. They were like a headstrong horse with a bit in his teeth, beyond holding in. The troops on the left had moved, and they did but keep up with the general movement. They had already shown emulation to dress up the lines, in conformity with the general alignment, and to be as far in advance as the others. They were restive and impatient at the delay and were filled with confidence and ardor. They had not been ordered to advance, but the order seemed to have been taken for granted and to have been a spontaneous intuition. What else were they there for? This was their fight; their officers had nothing to do with the advance.

The movement began in two lines, but the second to get under the dip of the batteries had closed up to the first. Thus they charged up the hill in the wildest enthusiasm. They would spring into the rifle-pits before the rebels could get out and make their escape and would press onward and upward, and encourage each other. That brave soldier and kind-hearted gentleman, Col. Carter, like the lamented Maj. Ellis, at Chickamauga, waved his hat to me as we climbed, and as I caught his beaming joyous eye, he fell, and to this day suffers from a grievous wound then and there received.

But I did not share in this hopeful confidence.

I had no misgivings about carrying the ridge, but in doing so the enemy would wrap his extended flank about us and we would be crushed and destroyed. And as I assisted myself over the obstacles of the way with my heavy sabre as a lever, I would exclaim to myself, "Good-by, my brave boys! good-by; you will gain the top, but it will be your last success; it will be the last of the First Brigade!" I felt like a lamb led to the slaughter, helpless and hopeless.

It was now growing dusk, and still our lines pressed forward. We did not delay longer under the fire of the enemy than was necessary to overcome the obstructions of the ascent, and did not attempt to return shot for shot, but the enemy continued to pour into us an incessant fire, however overshooting us, partly in order to avoid shooting their own men whom we closely followed up the hill, and partly from errors in judgment. At length the summit was reached, and the enemy fell back and made no further resistance, and my forebodings came suddenly to an end.

Soon after the enemy gave way, Osterhaus opportunely came up from Rossville, and obliquely approaching our right, joined us, thus forming an acute angle within the area of which the enemy was huddled together in great masses. They were anxious to surrender for the protection it gave them. Many officers would deliver up their swords to an orderly, or to any one who would take them. One of them claimed especial courtesy because the number of his regiment was thirty-eight, the same as mine. Four hundred prisoners, including one hundred and seventy commissioned officers, were hastily collected and sent to the city in a body, and the gun of our battery captured at Chickamauga was here retaken. The joy of the men knew no bounds and shouts and cheers filled the air and reached up and down the lines. Even the prisoners caught the excitement and yelled and gesticulated in the general rejoicing, and clasping our hands would assert, "You are cleverer fellows than we took you to be." Gen. Osterhaus threw up his cap and exclaimed, "Two more hours daylight and we'll destroy this army!" I, too, caught the infection and joined in the universal exultation. I had come up from the "Slough of Despond" and now revelled in the bright realms of hope and success. I seemed to have acquired another faculty, another sensation, the sense of victory! A verse of a hymn was recalled that in my boyhood I had heard my mother sing. The words are ascribed to Henry Kirk White. I have not seen or heard them since, but will quote from memory:

> "Earth has a joy unknown to Heaven,
> The new-born joy of sins forgiven;
> Tears of such rare and sweet delight,
> Oh, Angels, never dimmed your sight!"

The emotion of victory was a new-born joy. Its transports had suddenly overcome me with all the associations of conquests, the battle field and the captives.

A shanty was found near by and we established ourselves there for the night; our supper had been brought out to us from the town.

Two confederate officers had just been brought in and they were invited to share the meal. One of them, a major, took in the situation with composure and made himself agreeable. Of course, we avoided subjects which would mar the harmony and pleasure of the repast. But the other officer, a Lieut. Colonel, was sour, morose and forbidding. In reply to a question from Gen. Carlin as to his position in the army, and place of service, he said that he had served under Pemberton at Vicksburg. Carlin replied with some asperity that he was surprised to find him here again in arms, after having been paroled in the surrender to Grant. The colonel tartly replied, "My officers ordered me on duty; the propriety of the order I decline to discuss."

During the rejoicing, we did not abate our vigilance to secure the fruits of the victory, and reconnoitering parties came and went gathering up stragglers and disorganized bands. The next day reinforcements were sent to relieve Gen. Burnside, who was sorely pressed at Knoxville, and plans arranged for the pursuit of Bragg. Hooker was to attack the retreating column at Ringgold; Davis was to press them in the rear to Graysville, and Palmer was to strike them at intermediate points. The first brigade was in advance, and Palmer, Johnston, Carlin and myself rode at the head of the column. At length we turned off of the main road and entered a long, dark grotto. The road had been overflowed by a creek, which had subsided and left it with a cracked, glazed surface, and the branches of the trees joined over our heads.

We had not proceeded far when Gen. Palmer thus addressed us :

"Gentlemen, the success of this undertaking depends upon its being a surprise; therefore, send down the column and have the men cautioned not to speak above a whisper, and to move quickly and quietly, and above all, to keep well closed up."

Night had now come on and we marched through the woods until we at length came up to a road upon which the enemy were in full retreat. We proceeded quietly to form a line in the edge of the undergrowth which lined the road, and could hear the "gee-ups" and cracking whips of the artillery men and teamsters, and the slang and ribaldry of the rebel soldiers as they with unconscious abandon trudged along. There was a house on the roadside near the left of our line, which was filled with stragglers, who came and went as the retreating column passed along. One of my staff officers had opportunely surprised and detained the owner of this house at a gate a few feet from a side door. The man was disposed to give the alarm, but a pair of threatening pistols at his head admonished him to silence. In reply to my question as to whose troops these were, he replied in a whisper, as he was warned to do, "Gist's." Leaving a guard over the man and house, I hastened to one of the regiments which was not closed up, to urge them forward, and found the men picking theri way among the branches of the trees, which had been blown down and had so obstructed the drainage that water had collected about them. To avoid wetting their feet, the men were mincing their steps, thus impeding the rear and delaying the movement. No shouting or noisy demonstrations were permissible, with the necessity for quiet. So, bursting with indignation, I seized the shoulder of the officer in charge, and shaking him to arrest his attention, in a hoarse whisper, with "animated moderation," said to him,

"Will you convince me that you are fit to command men, that you have the stuff in you that influences men? If you have, prove it to me right here, and make your men walk through this water and close up the column." The water was walked in and the column closed up, but I did not need this to prove the efficiency of this gallant officer; I only relate it as a scene in this unique and dramatic situation.

And now all was ready; the culminating moment had come; a volley, a dash, one long, explosive shout and all was still again. The artillery teams and other *impedimenta* stood in the way, but such of the rebels as escaped shied into the woods on their left. They had only a short respite, for our line now wheeled to the left, our right sweeping the woods, while the left remained stationary on the road, and thus, like an immense seine, we gathered them in and directed them down the line to the pivot, where stood Palmer, Johnson and others to view the spectacle!

Gen. Johnson accosted one of them, a sprightly, soldierly fellow:

"Well sir, who and what are you?"

"I am a major in the Eighteenth South Carolina Infantry," was the prompt reply.

"Well, what do your people say about this little affair that has just come off?" continued Johnson.

The Major hesitated, and then answered, "We don't say much about it?"

Johnson continued, "Well, now, speak out;

did you whip us or did we whip you?" The Major, after a pause, replied,

"We think we had the advantage of your best troops," doubtless referring to Sherman's difficulties.

"Oh, they were just some of our Dutch we put in there," replied Johnson. This somewhat nonplussed the Major, but he rallied as he caught the General's drive and, determined not to be put down, shrugged his shoulders and replied,

"Well, we think *they are* your best troops."

Palmer applauded the answer and joked Johnson at the turn the colloquy had taken, and we were all, including the witty Major, in a good humor.

We now moved up the valley toward Graysville. Our lines were deployed and reached well across the valley, for we expected to meet Gen. Davis on the way, and thereby enclose other forces of the enemy between our lines. But Davis did not arrive at Graysville soon enough, or we were too soon, for the enemy took another road around the head of the ridge at Graysville and escaped.

But we were in time to save the wagon and railroad bridges over the Chickamauga. Both of these had been set afire, but were extinguished before much damage was done.

The men now lay down for a much-needed rest. Our party adjusted a rail fence so as to serve as a bed, and disposed ourselves to sleep. Gen. Palmer lay next to me and seemed restless. I asked him if he wanted anything, when he replied: "I don't like the appearance of things. Here is a town through which troops have been passing all night, and has now become all at once quiet and dark." I asked him if he would like to have the town patrolled, that there was a provost marshal and men to do it. He replied, "Yes, I would; but detail a regiment and have them search the place and find out what is in it."

When the patrol knocked at the doors of the houses, the yawning, sleepy inmates would protest against the intrusion — that they were tired and sleepy and did not wish to be disturbed; but the opening of the doors was insisted upon, and when they were finally opened, the rooms were found to be full of rebels. They were hid in closets, under the beds, and stowed away in all manner of concealment, and thus more prisoners fell into our hands. At this time, also, Gen. Palmer ordered a detail of four brave and discreet men to reconnoitre the country from the hills about us, and find out all they could concerning the route taken by the enemy in his retreat.

Early the next morning we continued the pursuit, moving south on the road east of us. We had not proceeded far when we found the mangled body of one of the four men detailed as scouts the night before. He was shot in several places and his face was horribly hacked with a saber. This brutality made the men feel ugly, and had they not been restrained, they would probably have retaliated upon the groups of rebels picked up from time to time as we marched along.

Approaching Ringgold, the noise of musketry and artillery indicated that Hooker was fighting a battle. It was here that the Seventh Ohio lost so heavily, their colonel and lieutenant-colonel both being killed.

At Taylor's Ridge we were again formed

in battle array. The railroad at the base of the ridge and a stream of water which flowed by, afforded protection to the enemy, who from the wooded hillside kept up a heavy fire upon us. To make a charge upon them we had to cross an open field, the stream and the railroad embankment; it was also desirable to extend our line farther to the right, but the creek ran through the field directly toward the right of our line. There was a footway across the creek some distance to the front composed of two large hewn logs laid side by side, so we advanced *en echelon* from the right. When the leading battalion came abreast the footway they promptly marched across by the flank and, facing to the front, opened their fire upon the enemy to protect in turn the passage of the next battalion. They marching in the rear of the first battalion, formed on their right, and thus the extension of the line was made while our flanks were protected and a constant fire kept up to the front. Having all crossed the creek, a charge was made and the enemy routed again.

I mention this movement in detail to illustrate an instance where the tactics fit all conditions, and where the lesson in the book was performed in battle with all the precision of the drill ground. We were occupied about Ringgold several days in reconnoitering and skirmishing, getting together the prisoners, collecting arms and accoutrements which were strewn over the ground, and then we returned to Chattanooga.

The First Division encamped on and about Cameron Hill. Gen. Carlin used the unoccupied Cameron House for his brigade headquarters, and soon afterward returned home on a short leave of absence, and I was left in charge of the brigade, but I continued thus only for a short time. The Thirty-eighth was transferred to the Third Brigade, which placed me in command, and I continued in command of this large and splendid brigade during the remainder of my term of service.

The picturesque scenery surrounding the spots where these grand and historic events transpired, renders the grounds about Chattanooga especially attractive and worthy of the pilgrimages made to them. Views of the landscape from the summit of Lookout Mountain and from points on Missionary Ridge, Orchard Knob and Cameron Hill afford a varied panorama of matchless sublimity and beauty. Some of the faces which Nature puts on, some of the smiles that radiate and adorn her features, are hidden from most men. But a very few have witnessed the splendor of the Aurora Borealis, the magical Mirage, or the wonderful transformations which obtain in certain localities, or have been in such *rapport* with their surroundings as to fully realize that they are communing with Nature. One morning, from the portico of the Cameron House, a scene was beheld by me the like of which I have never heard described. A silver mist had settled down over the entire valley, obscuring the city and all objects below the point on which I stood. Its margin was well defined and sharply cut against the elevations above its level. Its outlines followed all the sinuosities and intricacies above its surface, like a molten metallic mass. The sky above was of surprising clearness and brilliancy, and the sun shone out with all his glorious effulgence upon a vast sea of silver. Where this sea of silver overspread the river winding in the distance, it glistened with burnished brigntness.

This extraordinary vision suggested to the mind that prehistoric period when the vast glaciers were remodeling the surface of the earth and were breaking through the barriers which these very mountains opposed to the passage of the beautiful river which now winds its way in triumph among them. From beneath this silver sea could be heard the notes of the bugle and hum and noises of the city and camps below. These noises were loud, and the words spoken were audible and distinct, as if, like the actors in the vast amphitheaters of Greece and Rome, they spoke through trumpets to augment the power of their voices; or as if the floor of heaven had been lowered and the voices heard were those of Virgil and Dante on their celebrated inspection tour of the regions below. Or perhaps the mists had been condensed on the colder ground of the valley, and the dry air above formed a vast sounding-board which emphasized and propagated these mysterious reverberations.

But in the presence of such manifestations of nature, and with such examples of the visionary and marvelous set by her, one may take license to frolic in fantastic speculations.

CHAPTER VIII.

INCIDENTS BEFORE AND AFTER THE BATTLE.

ON THE 3d of November, the day Sherman crossed the Tennessee at Brown's Ferry, I was at Bridgeport, and suspecting from the movements and rumors that a battle was impending, I hurried back to Chattanooga to join in it, and crossed the river on the pontoons at Bridgeport. The flat-bottomed boats were anchored at regular intervals in a line with each other, and planks were laid from boat to boat to form the roadway. There were no side rails to give a feeling of security to a nervous person, and the surface of the road was but a few inches above that of the water, which splashed over it, as, roaring and boiling, it sped by. I had not passed more than half the distance over before a train of wagons was observed approaching, which gave me no little uneasiness, and when I came within hailing distance, I called out to the leading teamster to give me as much of the road as possible, but he paid no attention to my request and continued to come on in the middle of the road on which two teams could not pass each other. My horse began to shy and grow restive, and I became alarmed and feared being crowded off the bridge, or that my horse might be grazed by the teams, which would startle him and cause him to take to the river. But to my repeated appeals no attention was paid, and driven to desperation by the appalling situation, I took out one of my pistols from the holster and pointed it at the leading teamster, which together with my decorated language induced him to yield more of the road. My horse stood trembling with fear as the wagons passed, and I felt sure that had he been even touched by the passing train he would have plunged off the bridge.

I proceeded on my way and inquired the road to Brown's Ferry from the troops passing on the various roads. At times I would ride along with the troops, when their way and mine was the same. During the day I made the acquaintance of Major Thomas Acton, of the Fortieth Ohio Infantry, and was much taken with his handsome person and agreeable manners. After a long and pleasant chat we parted, shaking hands, and wished each other safely out of the coming battle. But my heartfelt wishes were of no avail, for the next night I beheld his lifeless form lying with the dead. My gallant major was among those we had cheered as they swung around the palisades on Lookout Mountain.

It was night before Brown's Ferry was reached. The bridge had just been swept away by the fallen trees and logs which either the rising river or the hands of the enemy had guided into the swollen current. The horse-boat had been ferrying over some of Sherman's staff officers, and now others were waiting to cross, but there was delay on account of the worn-out condition of the mules that propelled the boat. After a time other mules were obtained and placed in position to work. A man passed near me to cast off the rope which held the boat to the bank, and I asked him if he was the captain of the boat. He facetiously replied that he was "the aforesaid individual." I continued,

"Captain, pardon me for meddling with your business, but don't you think it would be well to try those fresh mules before you cast loose the boat from the bank? This is an ugly river and the whirlpool and suck are just below us."

The captain concluded it would be as well to try the mules first, and proceeded to do so; but no coaxing or beating would prevail upon them to budge; not a step would they take together around the circle to be trodden in order that the paddle wheel should turn over. The exhausted mules having been fed and rested, were again brought back and the crossing was safely effected.

I now made my way through Sherman's troops, who crowded the road up the river to the place they were to cross again to attack Bragg's right flank. I fortunately found the steamer "Dunbar," a little boat that had been constructed of odds and ends, and was taken at once on her to Chattanooga, and daylight found me at brigade headquarters, where after twenty-four hours of adventure, I flung myself down for a short sleep before entering upon the scenes of another day.

One night while we were waiting at Ringgold

to complete the work upon Bragg's retreating forces, a lot of officers were seated around a log fire, when an old colored man was observed circling about and gesticulating to attract our attention. At length Gen. Johnson spoke to him and drew him into the conversation. He was tall, slim and straight for one of his age, his white hair crisply curled in spots about his head and shriveled face. The old man interested us with his recollections of the past. He had seen Henry Clay, Gen. Jackson and other distinguished men, had formed many quaint and original opinions during his long and uneventful life, and withal quite a philosopher in his humble way. Among other things he said:

"My old massa is much discouraged; he is bin downhearted more'n a year, he did not want to put in a crap; he said what's th' use ter put in a crap, the Confederates will come an' git it, an' if they don't, the Yankees will. But I tell massa to put in the crap anyhow, and ef it was not tuck, we'd have the crap, an' spo'se it was took, we'd occupy de mind, occupy de mind," and in this way he talked on.

Gen. Palmer asked him what he thought about

the proclamation of Lincoln, setting the negroes free. His countenance assumed a gravity even greater than its wont, and looking into the fire as if thoughtfully turning the subject over in his mind, he replied, "I'se an old nigger an' my time will soon be gone; I can't work much any mo' I s'pos I'll have ter keep close ter my ole massa de res' o' my days." Then straightening himself up and closing his hands together, he threw back his head, and, gazing up at the stars as if all the beatitudes were filling his soul, passionately exclaimed, " But, oh, ef I wus on'y a young man, ef on'y I wuz a young man !" The pathos and the lesson it revealed deeply impressed us all.

I caught another glimpse of the inner life of the southern slave about this time. On coming out of my tent into the bright moonlight, I observed an old negro who served one of my staff officers. He was sitting down by the fire with his hands clasped about his knees. I accosted him with " Is that you, Joe? what time do you think it is?" Before replying he made a deliberate and careful survey of the heavens and then answered, " Its 'bout fo' 'clock in de mornin." I continued, "Joe, when I asked you what time it was why did you gaze up in the sky?" He replied, "Law, Massa, when a feller's sweetheart libs five miles off on anudder planta'shn, an' he has'tr be back agin' 'fo de bell ring in de mawnin', he mity soon learn to look up at de stars."

Soon after Gen. Carlin's departure on his leave of absence, one of his servants came to me for permission to go to McLemore's cave. I said to him, "Pete, I can't let you go there; it's beyond the pickets. What do you want to go there for?"

"I want to git my wife an' chile," he answered.

"Gen. Carlin left you in my charge, and you can't go. You might get into trouble there." Pete pleaded earnestly, but I was firm. At length he said, "I will tell you all about it. I was born on de same day as my young massa, and my old massa gib me to my young massa; my mammy nuss me an' him boff, and when he git bigger we play togedder an' fish an' hunt wid each udder. When young massa went norf to college I went wid him an' tended on 'im, an' when he went down to Mississippi state to buy de bit lands, I goed wid 'im; he had tents an' camp fixin's jes like de soljers, an' I cooked an' 'tended to things. When young massa went fur a kurnel in de army, I went too, an' when arter a long time massa git a furlo' to go home, I was mity glad, fur I wanted to see my wife and chilluns, jes de same as young massa did his'n. Now, what you think? When I got home I found my wife an' chilluns gone, sold! Young massa had his wife an' chilluns, but mine were gone, sold! I tell you what I was mighty mad, an' cut up bad about it! I told 'em I wouldn't be a good nigger any mo'. They tole me ef I didn't 'have they'd sell me, too. I tole 'em to sell, but I'd run away; an' I did run 'way, an' I fetched my wife to McLemore's cave, an' then cum'd you folks. Now I want to go an' git her. Yo' need'n be afeared, we darkies kno' how to do; I won't git kotched." This story touched the tenderest spot in me, and I told Pete he could go. And he went, and a few days afterward brought his wife and one of the children; a room was set apart for them in the house, and she was established as laundress at brigade headquarters.

Sitting one day in my office at brigade headquarters, I was not a little surprised to have Mr. Anderson announced. After cordial greetings on both sides, the old gentleman made known to me his errand.

"Would you believe it," said he, " I have not seen my Mary since she left me when you all came. When Bragg left Chattanooga she went on to Calhoun, and I want to go there for her: I want her home; so I thought I would ask you to help me to get a pass."

I did not think it possible to get the old gentleman through the lines, but I wanted to be kind to him, and replied that I knew Col. Wiles, the provost marshal, very well, and would write him a letter in his behalf, and remarked, as I drew the writing material toward me, "But, Mr. Anderson, you are too old a man for a soldier."

"But I don't intend to be a soldier," said he.

"But you might be drafted when you arrive at Calhoun," I replied. He became excited and rejoined,

"Tut, tut, they would not draft an old man

like me into the Confederate army, would they?"

"I don't know what they will do, but I will tell you what I do know. Among the prisoners we brought from Ringgold the other day, there were several men older than you are, and I had to threaten and shame the younger men to make them assist some of the old and feeble ones along." Mr. Anderson then changed his mind about going to Calhoun, and said:

"You need not write any letters about it." He then went on to describe the changes which had taken place since I left Anderson.

"You wouldn't know the place; troops marching through it or stopping for a few days have stripped it of fences, stock and out-houses, and it looks like a ruin. But I want to ask you how I am to get paid for corn taken when I have no vouchers to show. I understand all about those you gave me—they are all right; but when a wagon-master comes along and fills his wagons and gives me no ticket, how will I get pay for that?" I replied:

"Well, Mr. Anderson, I will answer your question by asking you one; if before the war you woke up and found your stable door open and your horses gone, what would you have done?"

"I should have had to find the thief or the horses. Yes, yes; I see. That corn is lost, for I could never trace the men who took it, nor identify the corn."

I felt truly sorry for the old man. All his gorgeous hopes in the Southern Confederacy had been dispelled and he had, instead, nothing but disaster and loss to look upon.

One day Lieut.-Col. Griffin called upon me and remained to dinner. I knew from his manner that he had something on his mind to talk about. He had a feminine way of putting off the main subject until the last moment, to be incidentally referred to. At length it came out; he opened the subject by remarking, "Gen. Wilder has returned."

"Well, what has he to say," said I.

"The General has been requested by Gov. Morton to call upon all the Indiana regiments whose term of service is about to expire, with a view to having them reënlist for three years longer, or during the war," the Colonel replied.

"Has he called upon the Thirty-eighth yet?" I asked.

"Yes," was the Colonel's reply.

"Well, what do the boys say about it?" I asked.

"They ask what does the old Colonel say about it," the Colonel replied.

After a pause I continued: "What do you say about it?"

He promptly replied, "I ask, like the boys, 'What does the old Colonel say about it?'"

This brought the subject home to me and forced me to speak of a subject rarely alluded to, yet one I felt sorely about. At last I opened my heart to hin

"Dan, I will tell you just how I feel concerning this matter. My promotion is very doubtful. You know my name has several times been sent by Mr. Lincoln to the Senate for confirmation, but they adjourn without taking it up, or say there are no vacancies. I have no political friends, with, perhaps, the exception of Gov. Morton, to press my claim, so I begin to feel that I am but a stumbling-block for others. Now, you have been performing the duties of the colonel of the regiment for a long while with the rank and pay of only a lieutenant-colonel. I have about made up my mind that the proper and decent thing for me to do would be to resign and give others a chance."

The Colonel flashed up and curtly replied, "When you quit, I quit."

Here was my old dilemma again, not to serve myself and yet prevent others, for I knew the men would hesitate to muster again with such examples before them, and thus the cause would be robbed of the services of a body of men who had been tried and found true. I therefore replied, "Dan, if you talk in that way, I have no choice but to remain."

He resumed: "Will you come and tell the men so?"

I replied, "Yes."

"When?" persisted the Colonel.

"Whenever you say," I answered.

The Colonel, as if he feared to risk me, said, "I say now. Will you come now?" I had been well handled and was committed; so the horses were ordered and we rode off together to his quarters at Rossville. On the way I was informed how the men talked among themselves on the subject, and of the differences of opinion between them. Thirteen students from the northern part of our State came down to New Albany, and were mustered in as private soldiers with the regiment when it was organized. They were a fine body of young men, and would do honor to any company or any cause. These men seemed disinclined to reënlist, and the Colonel wished me to speak especially to them, for they wielded great influence on the others. So they were sent for. Their spokesman, in reply to my question concerning their feelings on the subject, said they had lost nearly three important years, and if they carried out the plans of their lives, as they had marked them out, they should not further delay the finishing of their course of study, if they expected to enter upon their professions with fair chances of success.

    I replied that I would not oppose the justice of their view, and if I thought they would go ho e and carry them out, not another word would be said by me. "But you will not be able to settle down to study while this struggle, in which you have borne so honorable a part, is yet in progress. Once a soldier always a soldier. A man who had once been a soldier was like one bitten by a mad dog. It is said that one so bitten will have recurrences of the symptoms at the sight of water. So it will be with you at the sight of a recruiting station. The flag and music of the fife and drum will irresistibly draw you and awaken all the old associations of your army life, so that in a few weeks you will be off again in the One Hundred and Fiftieth or some other high-numbered regiment. Now, having cast your lot with the Thirty-Eighth, which has earned a reputation we were all so proud of, I submit to you the question, is it not better to stay with the grand old regiment the short time yet that the rebellion will be able to hold out than to hazard your fame in a new and untried one?"

They concluded to stay with the regiment and reënlisted with it for three years more, if the war should last that long.

Several of these men were promoted during the war for meritorious service. David H. Patton, who was one of the renowned color-guard that survived the battle of Perryville, afterward became captain, and when Low was killed at

Bentonville, the last battle in which the Thirty-eighth fought, Capt. Patton became colonel of the regiment, and was afterward a brigade commander. This shows the vicissitudes of war.

To illustrate the influence for good or evil a few men can exert over a command, I will refer to a slight collision I once had with my division commander.

He had detailed ten men to work in the quartermaster's department, and specified the persons by name. I sent ten men, but not the ones called for in the requisition. The General sent for me and took me to task for disregarding his order. I replied in defense that, while I recognized his right to call upon me for men, I thought that I should be consulted in regard to who could be best spared for the purpose required, for ten men could be picked from any company in the service, and the status of the company thereby changed and perhaps its efficiency destroyed; that ten men gave character and tone to every company. This known and controlled, the management of the rest became easy. The General was too old and good a soldier not to see the force of my position, and at once approved my action. If those who have the management of large bodies of workmen would consider the subject in this way, many strikes might be avoided.

There are also distinctions between officers. I do not refer to the apparent ones of good and bad, but I mean there is a difference between brave and capable ones. For example, an officer has been sent to protect a bridge or ford; it is not a desirable place to be, and it will not be long before complaints of the hardships his men are enduring will be heard; perhaps he will himself describe the deplorable situation and ask to be relieved. Now, while this officer will faithfully perform his duty until relieved, he will not spare his efforts for the change, and his commander may grant his request in consideration for him, and perhaps disturb his plans thereby.

Another officer in the same situation, who has come with a report, or for instructions, or with suggestions to make, will say that, while it is a rough place, yet "I think you had better keep me there, for we have learned the lines of fire of the enemy's sharpshooters, which would cause several lives of the force which should relieve me to learn." In this way good officers differ. And now, while it is true that a free horse will be ridden, yet, as Gen. Carlin says in his letter of farewell to Col. Griffin, "If you have been called upon to do more than your share, you may be sure that your commanding officer felt that the duty would be well done when performed by you." This, I think, would compensate a good soldier for any extra hardship he might have put upon him.

There seems to be a natural antipathy between a colonel and a lieutenant-colonel. I refer to the offices, not to individuals. The command of a regiment is not apportioned out among the field officers, but resides solely in the colonel; he commands the regiment and every one in it! But the colonel absent, then the same authority devolves upon the lieutenant-colonel. Now, it often happens that these officers are detailed on various duties and at different times, which separates one or more of them from the regiment. Then all the gossips, talebearers and toadies will set to work to estrange them from each other. The absent one will be criticised by inuendoes, so far as the dignity of the officer will permit them to go, and provided also the officer is weak enough to allow himself to be approached in this way by any one.

When the lieutenant-colonel assumes command in the absence of the colonel, smirking faces will tell him how happy the men are at the change, and he will begin to pity them that they cannot have him always over them. When the colonel returns, other smirking faces will express their joy at his return to correct the abuses that have grown in his absence, and he will feel sorry that for their sake he cannot always be with them. If there are any weak spots in the character of the field officers, there will be Iagos enough to find them. I suppose it is the same frailty of human nature that creates the antagonisms said to exist between the sovereign and his heir. I refer to this matter to more strongly bring out the beauty and symmetry of the character of Col. Griffin.

In private life he was a civil engineer; his form was slight and his manner quiet and unobtrusive; he seldom talked, but was a good listener; his intelligent countenance showing that he always fully comprehended what others were saying. I never heard him laugh, but his expressive eyes could laugh and dance, too, in the merriment that others were boisterously enjoying. His character was pure; he was gentle and refined, and if he was living alone in a cave, he would eat like a gentleman. I never heard him use a profane or indelicate word, yet he was not prudish or censorious of others. He was a good disciplinarian, yet not tyrannical or overbearing, but when he did move upon a wrong-doer, there was no let-up until the culprit was crowded to the wall; and while from the reticence of his disposition he may not have said what he thought, he always meant what he said. In battle he was calm and undemonstrative; did not shout himself hoarse to enthuse the men, but with serenity and repose was wherever it was his duty to be, even though it was in the thickest of the fight. He seemed to bear a charmed life, and it was a cause of wonder how he ever got out alive from some of his perilous situations. His horses were shot, his clothes torn by bullets, but blood was drawn from him but once, and this was more by accident than from any especial danger in his locality. I had asked him to assist me to determine the direction of the works of the enemy and the location of our forces, as I expected soon to be ordered to relieve one of the brigades in our division. The colonel was a good woodsman, which I was not. While he was pointing out the intricacies of ridge and ravine, a partly-spent ball struck him in the breast, and plunging through the wadding of his regulation uniform coat, which he in all kinds of weather wore buttoned up to the chin, and cutting through shirt and undershirt, broke the skin of his bony chest and brought a show of blood. I picked up the bullet for him, and, as he took it, remarked, that as he was here on my business, he would send the bill for mending the coat to me for payment. The Thirty-eighth was blessed in having such a painstaking and capable officer. It was especially a thing for me to be grateful for, to have so faithful and sincere a successor; we never differed and were always in harmony with each other. He manifested a delicacy in always consulting me about promotions and other internal matters in the regiment, for a colonel, detached from his regiment and in command of a brigade, has in reality no more to say or do with his own regiment than he has with any other in the brigade. Yet he is borne upon its rolls, and all his rank and authority proceeds from his position on them, and his honor and standing are identified with it. Hence it is very easy for an illy disposed lieutenant-colonel to mortify and wound the feelings of the colonel so situated. But Griffin was above all such inconsiderate actions.

In concluding this honest tribute to this heroic soldier and gentleman, I will here add that after long and faithful service his health broke down and he was forced to resign, and in a few months after his return home he lay down in his bed and quietly passed away like a private citizen.

When the Thirty-eighth went home on the thirty days' furlough granted to regiments that enlisted, I went with them. Gen. Thomas was very considerate in relieving all officers and men on detached service, so that they could not only enjoy their visit together, but would also be able to more effectively obtain recruits for their thinned ranks.

There were some peculiar conditions attending this furlough of the Thirty-eighth that may be of interest to note.

On returning to one's home after a long absence and from different environments, there is generally a gradual approach. Familiar objects one by one successively meet the eye and prepare one for the change. But the Thirty-eighth was shut up in box-cars and rushed through to Louisville with only such stops as were necessary for the train to make for wood and water. They arrived at Louisville before daylight and crossed the river to New Albany early in the morning. And now a sudden change transforms the scene. The bank of the river was lined with the loyal citizens, who received the war-worn veterans with every demonstration of joy and welcome; flags and handkerchiefs waved, guns fired, drums beat and bands of music played to greet them. The streets were alive with happy people. Friends and relatives from the surrounding country had gathered here and swelled the crowd, and for a time impeded all progress. In a large hall, beautifully decorated with flags and flowers, were rows of tables covered with creature comforts. Into this room they were conducted, and at those tables the hungry men sat down. No change from army rations at eating-places on the route had modified the zest with which those viands were relished. This was the first coffee they had drank since they left their camp at Rossville. The cold contents of their haversacks was their only larder on the way. It was as if they had closed their eyes surrounded by privations, hardships and neglect, and had opened them in Elysium, where they were kindly ministered to by loving friends. They had for nearly three years been deprived of the comforts of home; had been in, to them, a strange land among hostile people; had marched over more than 2,000 miles of the enemy's country; had passed through the fiery ordeal of many battles, and now, as if it were in a moment, the twinkling of an eye, they had been magically transported to the blessed endearments of home. And at their homes let us leave them to enjoy the comforts they have so faithfully earned, for in thirty days they must again take up the role of a soldier's life.

CHAPTER IX.

THE ATLANTA CAMPAIGN.

ARLY in the spring of 1864 preparations for renewing operations upon the enemy occupied the minds of those in command. Grant was now commander-in-chief of the Union armies. Henceforth Lee was not to be permitted to reinforce one of his armies from another on his interior lines of communication, but was to be so vigorously and simultaneously assaulted by us at all points that his forces would all be employed in defending themselves, and therefore unable to give assistance to others.

Sherman succeeded Grant in command of the Military Division of the Mississippi. His forces consisted of the Army of the Cumberland, under Gen. Thomas; the Army of the Tennessee, under Gen. McPherson; and the Army of the Ohio, under Gen. Schofield.

General Joseph E. Johnston had succeeded Bragg, and was at Dalton, and had advance troops at Rocky-face and Buzzard Roost mountains.

Sherman delayed his movement in order to discover the intentions of the enemy under their new commander. For a time there were indications that he intended to move to our flank and rear in East Tennessee, but on the 7th of May Sherman had formed his plans and was ready to move upon Johnston.

I was now in command of the Third Brigade, same division and corps as before, which was composed of the First Wisconsin, under Lieut.-Col. Bingham; Twenty-first Wisconsin, under Lieut.-Col. Hobart; Twenty-first Ohio, under Col. Neibling; Seventy-fourth Ohio, under Col. Given; Twenty-fourth Illinois, under Col. Miholatzy; Thirty-seventh Indiana, under Lieut.-Col. Ward; Seventy-eighth Pennsylvania, under Col. Wm. Sirwell; Seventy-ninth Pennsylvania, under Col. Hambright, and Thirty-eighth Indiana, under Lieut.-Col. Griffin.

As the campaign progressed, one or more of the regiments were from time to time temporarily detached on various duties. The artillery were not permanently assigned to brigades, but were under the brigade commander within whose lines for the time being they chanced to be.

Sherman now had about one hundred thousand men, most of whom were veterans just returned from their furloughs. The Army of the Cumberland made more than one half of Sherman's force. The hundred regiments of veterans had brought over eight thousand recruits with them when their thirty days' furlough expired. These new men, distributed among the old soldiers, readily assimilated, and soon became as effective as their more experienced comrades.

I will here call the attention of the critics who, during the war. found so much fault with the authorities at Washington for their management of affairs, and ask them to consider the neglect of the rebel leaders to improve an occasion when our army was stripped of nearly all the old soldiers going home on veteran furlough, and try, if they can, to explain or excuse it.

On the 7th of May we advanced from Ringgold, and our skirmishers were soon employed. On the next day we were in line before Buzzard

Roost. Obstructions had been placed in Mill Creek by the enemy, which caused it to overflow the road to Dalton between Buzzard Roost and Rocky-face. We were at once subjected to a vigorous resistance from the enemy, and heavy firing from artillery and musketry soon made it apparent that the enemy were prepared for us.

Gen. Thomas had before made a reconnoissance in force and knew the difficulties to be overcome in assailing this stronghold. Gen. Carlin forded Mill Creek and advanced over a green slope up to the base of the mountain. My brigade was afterward ordered to do the same and connect with his left. We deployed in two lines. The creek was lined on both sides with bushes. We crossed by the right of companies, and as soon as we emerged from the cover of the bushes the enemy opened a terrific fire upon us from heavy guns on the mountain. This was wholly unexpected by us, for Carlin performed the same movement a few minutes before and not a shot was fired at him. They had been ordered to hold their fire, and permission had only been obtained when my troops showed themselves. The men behaved handsomely and the lines were perfect, and as they continued to advance, I thought I had never witnessed a finer sight or better marching on the parade ground. Here and there in our wake the grass was dotted with the prostrate slain, their blue coats contrasting with the verdant field.

I now noticed that one of the regiments on the flank remote from me was yet marching to the right of companies to the front, instead of having been promptly brought into line again after the creek was crossed. Thus they were in great danger of a raking fire in the flank. I shouted to the officer in command to bring his companies into line again, but could not make him hear me, so I dashed down the line myself to rectify so gross a blunder. My staff officers all followed after me. The whole scene was so much like a drill that they failed to consider that such an imposing cavalcade could not fail to attract the attention of the enemy and bring down upon us all their sharpshooters, in addition to the shot and shell from the batteries on the mountain. We all had to run the gauntlet before we could screen ourselves at the base of the mountain at Carlin's left. We were now under the dip of the guns on the mountains, but my men had no sooner reached this expected shelter than they were raked by a flank fire from batteries on the left. The ranges of fire of the sharpshooters required much study to discover their source, and only in certain locations could spots be found where their bullets would not find some of us or come whizzing by in unpleasant proximity. I felt as if we were being punished with our hands tied. There was no enemy here that we could reach. The mountain was covered with a dense forest. A ridge which appeared to lead to the summit would end in a ravine, and this crossed to the acclivity beyond. The discovery would be made that this too was divided by another ravine, and after this labarynth had been explored, we found ourselves in contact with a rocky precipice along which two men could not walk abreast. The absurdity of beating out our brains against these walls was soon manifest, and I so reported the situation to Gen. Whipple, chief of staff to Gen. Thomas. I did not know then that Sherman was only feigning to enable McPherson to attack Johnston in the rear from Snake Creek Gap.

We were so much annoyed by the sharpshooters, who became more and more troublesome, that the regimental commanders were ordered to select their best marksmen and have them investigate the points from which these shots proceeded, and at night throw up breastworks of stone, and before daylight with rations take possession of them and try to remedy the evil. Col. Hambright, of the Seventy-ninth Pennsylvania, was wounded here and was borne from the field. Capt. Van Dusen, a promising young officer of the Thirty-eighth, was struck on the foot in my presence. Col. Miholatzy, of the Twenty-fourth Indiana, was also wounded here and died a few days after. As my cook was serving the coffee, the pot was perforated by a bullet and the contents lost.

In camp, before these operations began, I made requisition for some loose cartridges which we found could be drawn. I wanted to determine some question my men had raised. They complained that our ammunition was not as good as that of the enemy. Ours was a black, sooty powder, while the enemy's was in shiny steel-colored grains. They therefore would increase the powder in their cartridges to render them more effective. They also objected to the sights of their guns, and thought they were incorrect. To settle these questions by experiments a suitable spot between two ridges was selected. Targets the size of a man were placed in position and rifle-pits were dug in front of them to protect the person who filled the bullet holes and reported the shots. The distances from the target of one, two, three, five hundred, and a thousand yards were carefully measured, and after several days of practice and application of careful tests, the conclusion was reached that both the powder and sights were right, and that by using them as the Ordnance Department furnished them, the best result would be obtained. The effect of these exercises upon the men was good, and gave them confidence in their means of defense. To stimulate them to strive to excel, I recommended to regimental commanders to have the names of the best shots read upon dress-parade. Accordingly, the next morning our sharpshooters went to work and soon conquered a peace, and we could walk about at will without a bullet whizzing about our ears. All the talk among the men of the enemy's splendid globe-sighted rifles, which could, with precision, send a bullet a thousand yards, now ceased, and they found they could do as much execution as the enemy. After our boys found the tree in which the rebel sharpshooter was located, they did not fail to roust him out of it.

After we had disposed ourselves out of range of the enemy's artillery, they ceased to fire at us, and our horses were sent to a wooded slope near the creek to graze and for shelter. There had been a heavy cannonading in this place, and we lost some men there. Barney Doyle, a private in the Thirty-eighth, was placed in charge of the horses. He was a brave and faithful soldier. While ascending Missionary Ridge he was wounded in the hand; but, notwithstanding, continued to push on until another shot struck him in the eye and brought him down. The ball, however, took one of those strange freaks which defy explanation, and passed upward between the scalp and skull and did him no serious injury. When Barney was asked why he did not go to the rear when his hand was shot, he replied, "How could I, when the Colonel said 'Forward'?"

The next morning, when the horses were sent

for, they were not at the place where they were expected to be, and only after much search could they be found. Barney was sent for and reproached by his Colonel for deserting his trust. He replied, "But it got dark." Griffin rejoined, "Because night came on made no difference; you should have stayed with the horses." When Barney, with a terror-stricken countenance, exclaimed, "What! with all those dead men lying about!" Poor, superstitious Barney! He was not afraid of live men, but the fear of the ghosts of dead ones fairly curdled his blood.

Among the wounded at Buzzard's Roost was one, concerning whom it may be of interest to relate an incident.

While we were encamped at Green River, near the beginning of our service, one of my captains, returning from recruiting-service, brought back with him ten recruits. At that time colonels of regiments were authorized to muster in enlisted men, so the Captain brought them to me for this purpose. All were accepted but one, and when this one was told to stand aside—that he was not suitable for a soldier—his face assumed an expression of mingled surprise and disappointment.

The Captain, also, did not expect this rejection. It was explained to him that the man had no front teeth, and therefore could not tear a cartridge or properly masticate his food, upon which the health of the soldier so much depended; and that the regulations made this man an improper one to muster, and further, that at any time a discharge could be obtained upon such a defect.

After the battle of Perryville, while we were at Crab Orchard and in pursuit of Bragg, I observed among a group surrounding a campfire a face with something familiar in it, and asked the Adjutant if he was not the toothless man I had refused to muster. Receiving an affirmative reply, the officer in command of the company was sent for and I inquired what that man was doing here, and was informed that he refused to go home; that he cooked for his mess, and the boys paid him a trifle for this service. It was developed that the man was detailed for guard or any other duty the rest of the company performed. But when the officer spoke of his good conduct in the late battle, my interest in him was increased. I asked the officer. "Does this man know that he draws no pay, and if he should be wounded he would draw no pension?" The officer replied, "Oh, yes; all this has been explained to him, but he won't go away." I determined at once to disregard all technicalities, and had the man brought up, and he was duly mustered into the service of the United States, and dated back to our last muster for pay. Now this brave fellow made a point, after each battle in which the regiment was engaged, to loiter about my quarters until he succeeded in attracting my attention, whereupon he would display his toothless mouth and point to his red gums, and then double himself up and sway his arms and body as if he was wrestling with a joke too huge to be controlled, and then, in great glee, would hasten away. He never sought to make my acquaintance or ask for a favor or even speak to me, and when I accosted him and was disposed to talk to him, he would not stop, being too full of the joke he had on me. To be thought unfit for a soldier for lack of teeth was to him very funny, and he was determined after each battle to remind me of my error, and by his toothless gums prove it to me. He was a happy, comical fellow, and soon recovered from his wound and went through with the regiment to the sea, and passed in grand review before the President and his Cabinet at Washington, after Lee's surrender.

We remained at Buzzard's Roost from the 8th to the night of the 12th, when we were relieved by Gen. Whittaker, and on the morning of the 13th we passed Snake Creek Gap, where we met the litter bearing off Gen. Kilpatrick, who had just been wounded in a severe fight in which he drove Wheeler's cavalry from their position. I also here made the acquaintance of the much-loved McPherson, Gen. King taking me to call upon him.

The enemy had now fallen back from Dalton to their works at Resaca, which had been constructed beforehand. We were soon in line advancing upon him. They yielded the ground from point to point only after stubborn resistance. During the day I met Gen. Thomas, and was introduced by him to Gen. Sickles of the Army of the Potomac, who was with him. They both seemed pleased with the way my lines advanced and drove the enemy.

Next day our division gained position close up to the fortifications of the enemy. McPherson had also advanced to the works at Resaca on the extreme right. Hooker joined us on our right; Carlin was on the right of our division. It now became necessary to swing round our left with our division as the pivot, in order to locate the enemy's works. The assault was successively made from the left to the right of our division. When Carlin moved forward I was ordered to be ready to support him, and moved my command down the ravine on each side of the wooded ridge, while I went in person down the ridge, the most direct but most difficult way to Carlin's position. The ridge ended in a bluff descent, and formed the right bank of Camp Creek. Carlin had just moved upon the enemy, and was at once vigorously resisted. Already the disabled were straggling back from his lines. My men were not up yet, and every minute seemed an hour to me. My relief was great when I discerned them approaching as fast as the obstacles of the way permitted. They at once proceeded to improve the defenses which Carlin had hastily thrown up, but the attack from our left did not prove to be continuous, and Carlin did not succeed in carrying the rebel works, although Hooker's artillery assisted him with heavy cross fire, in a manner characteristic of Gen. Hooker. But the object was attained, Howard and Schofield making great progress; and Johnston, fearing that his right would be turned, massed a heavy force upon Howard's thin lines, and Hooker reinforced him with his first division under that veteran soldier, Gen. A. S. Williams, who arrived just in time to prevent a disaster. Howard's left had not been able to withstand the shock and had already given way, but Williams regained the lost ground. Johnston tried this again the next day, but Gen. Williams, who seems up to this time to have had to bear the brunt of the fight, met the charge, and, together with Gen. Geary, retaliated with such vigor that Johnston was again foiled with heavy loss. At times the combat extended all along the line, and the discharges of artillery and musketry were terrible and destructive. During the night of the 15th Johnston made another furious assault upon our entire front, but was again repelled. On the morning of the 16th the enemy was gone and Resaca evacuated. It was very unfortunate that a decisive battle could not have been fought here. Many considerations made it desirable that Johnston should be prevented from crossing Oostenaula River. If McPherson could have carried out Sherman's plan and interposed between the enemy and his lines of communication, and thereby forced him to fight or to retreat eastward where he could not have supplied himself, a long and arduous campaign would have been avoided.

On paper this would seem easy to do with the forces at Sherman's command. That it was not done is to me proof that it was impracticable, for if the obstacles could have been overcome, the great ability and courage of those charged with the duty is a guarantee that it would have been done.

The country surrounding Resaca is broken with hills, ridges and ravines. It is densely wooded, and there were no roads available in the direction the enemy's position forced us to take in order to reach him. Johnston, on the other hand, had his defenses and roads already constructed, and could fall back from Dalton in the night and occupy them, when we had to find him by careful, laborious skirmishing. His positions were selected with a view of subjecting us to every danger and disadvantage. But I will not argue this question. Johnston got away from us and we did the next best thing in our power, and followed close upon his heels. His rear was well covered, he had several fortified lines from which his rear guard could retard our pursuit, and when routed from one position, fell back to another. At times these encounters were very severe.

CHAPTER X.

THE ATLANTA CAMPAIGN CONTINUED.

GEN. J. C. DAVIS was dispatched to demonstrate upon Rome, Ga. The city fell into his hands with much war material. The founderies and manufacturing establishments were all destroyed. Sherman doubtless hoped by moving upon Rome to induce Johnston to defend it or to fight him north of the Etowah River. But he moved toward the Altoona Mountain, yielding to us Calhoun, Adairsville, Cassville, Rome and Kingston. At Kingston Sherman lingered a few days, to collect supplies and prepare for a further advance.

In order to avoid the strong defensive position on Johnston's line of retreat, Sherman made a detour to the right toward Burnt Hickory and Dallas, intending to connect again with his railroad at Ackworth after Johnston had been outflanked from his stronghold at Altoona Pass. But Johnston suspected Sherman's design, and, to annoy or frustrate him, massed a heavy force upon McPherson at Dallas, and thereby was able to detain Sherman for several days, and frequent combats for position occurred. Several ineffectual efforts were made by McPherson to move to the left in order that we might reach our railroad. But Johnston kept such a close watch upon his movements and assaulted him so vigorously both by day and by night each time he made an effort to release himself from a position in which he seemed to be held as in a vise, that McPherson was forced to defend himself where he was, and wait the relief that other movements which would draw off the forces in his front would afford.

On the 27th of May, Sherman wished to find the right of the enemy's fortifications, and Gen. Howard undertook the task with Gen. Wood's division of the Fourth Corps, supported by the first division of the Fourteenth Corps. We moved cautiously all day in the dense woods, alternately to the front and then by the left flank, as we found the ever-present rebel breastworks. Gen. Johnson, our division commander, was an accomplished soldier and a refined and genial gentleman, but his patience here became exhausted. He rode up to me, with a bland courtesy that was in an inverse ratio with his displeasure—for, like the boatswain in Captain Marryat's "Peter Simple," he was politest when he was most dangerous. The conclusion of the General's complimentary and courteous address was, "Will you be so kind as to move due south until I tell you to halt?" I answered that I would do so, and proceeded to move as directed. I employed Lieut. Dewey, an efficient and dashing officer of my staff, to assist Col. Griffin in keeping me in that direction. They with their compasses in hand guided my movements. To comply with the orders of the General, we had to march through the lines of the troops in our front, which was a rude thing to do. But as I had no choice in the matter, we proceeded to march due south in two deployed lines, scattering apologies right and left as we passed through the lines of the surprised and offended troops. At length the front was gained, and, straightening up my line, we continued to move on until we came up to Gen. Howard, whom we recognized by his armless sleeve. The General was alone with his glass in hand surveying the front. I mollified his surprise and perhaps his displeasure at seeing me, by repeating to him my orders from my commanding officer. He desired me to communicate with Gen. Johnson and inform him that the rebel works were in our front and that it would be unsafe to advance farther to the front, and that he should now move again to the left. Gen. Johnson now rode up, and I left them in consultation, and soon the tedious movement to the left and to the front was continued. The day was hot; not a breath of air seemed to move in the dense undergrowth of the forest, and it was late in the afternoon when Howard concluded he had found the right of the enemy's works.

Gen. Wood's division was formed in six lines, and occupied a wooded knoll which hid them from view of the enemy. In Gen. Wood's front was a wheat-field, which sloped up toward a ridge covered with trees. On their left was Pumpkinvine Creek, which flowed tortuously at the base of a precipitous hill. Between Wood's left and the creek there was not room for me to form on their left, as directed, without throwing my left forward and thereby exposing the movement to the enemy. I had, therefore, no alternative but to bring up my two lines by the flank perpendicular to the front, so that they could be moved up into line after the movement commenced. The creek bore away to the left, and more room to extend the lines was obtained as the assaulting column advanced. My orders were to form on the left of Knefler, the rear brigade, and this was afterward changed to Gibson's, and to protect the flank of the assaulting column. When the division debouched from their cover, they were subjected to a vigorous fire from the enemy on the ridge. This increased as we advanced; artillery being added to the defense made by the enemy. My command rapidly prolonged the line as they found room to do so in the face of a terrific fire of musketry and artillery. The enemy fell back up the ridge and sought refuge behind their everattending breastworks. It was, however, soon manifest that our assault was a failure. A force of Schofield had been ordered to demonstrate on our right to mislead the enemy. This they failed to do; therefore, instead of finding the rebels unprepared for us, we found them ready with artillery and fortifications. They had evidently been made aware of our intentions in time to mass their forces to meet us. Where the attacking column halted, the dense forest prevented me from observing their situation, and my own required all my care and attention. For we were subjected to a galling and destructive fire on the flank, which forced me to send regiment after regiment to extend my left to protect it until I had but the Seventy-fourth Ohio, Col. Given, in the second line. My first line connected with and extended to the first line of the assaulting column, and, thus disposed, a severe battle was fought for several hours into the night. About ten o'clock the rebels raised their characteristic yell and rushed upon us. Their charge extended all along our line. My men did not yield an inch, but maintained their position behind such defenses as they had been able to hastily throw up. After a lull in the firing, shadowy objects were observed moving to the rear of my right, and, hastening to learn their purport, I met Col. Stout, of the Seventeenth Kentucky, whom

I had long known as a meritorious officer, and asked him what they were doing. He replied that they had been ordered to fall back. This irritated me not a little, and I tartly replied, "I think you might have had the courtesy to notify your supports of such a movement." To which the Colonel rejoined, "I know nothing about it; I am only obeying orders in falling back."

Soon my mind was made up what to do. Col. Given was a brave and intelligent officer. He was ordered to promptly deploy his regiment so as to cover the ground thus vacated, to slightly refuse his right, and not to be aggressive and bring on a fight, but to see that the enemy did not discover the absence of the force which had been in their front. It was explained to the Colonel and to all the regimental commanders that the enemy would not assail us again until they had carefully felt their way, and if we had to yield ground, they were to change fronts to the rear on the left battalion. By this movement they would be placed along the creek and would unmask the fire of King, who had now occupied the wooded knoll where Wood's division was massed and where the assault began. Thus they and King would have a cross-fire upon the enemy should he attempt to cross the wheat-field.

When Gen. Johnson observed the troops falling back and his brigade not among them, he was concerned for our safety, and sent a staff officer to investigate the situation. When he found us, I explained the state of affairs and sent by him reassuring messages to the General. The officer soon returned, saying that the General wished me to get my wounded back to the rear in the wheat-field, and then report the fact to him. It was not long, however, before the staff officer came again and said that the General was impatient at my delay. He was sent back with the message that his order had been delivered to the regimental commanders, and that when they reported they had complied with it, I would notify him. The officer was urged to relieve the General's anxiety by repeating to him my orders to the troops, and intended disposition of them in case we should be again assaulted in force. But the officer again returned with peremptory orders to return at once, and if I could not bring off my skirmish line to leave it. But I did not have to suffer this to be done. Maj. Bonafon, of the Seventy-Eighth Pennsylvania, who was known to be a skillful light-infantryman, was sent for, and the command of the skirmishers was intrusted to him. He was charged to be cautious and yet to be sufficiently aggressive, and to retire in alternate lines and to commence the movement when he saw us well into the wheat-field. Thus we got off safely. When the enemy discovered the movement they opened upon us with their artillery, but they were too late about it to seriously impede or injure us.

When we reached the wooded knoll we were cordially received by our comrades of the first and second brigades of our division, who congratulated us as if we had just escaped from the jaws of death. Gen. Johnson was especially pleased, and warmly greeted us. He was gratified that one of his brigades which was only expected to support the movement should have borne so important a part in the charge, and, after they had been abandoned by the assaulting column, held the position and afterward withdrew at their leisure, bringing off killed, wounded and prisoners. This was something which he considered very creditable, and next day he showed his appreciation of the conduct of the troops by issuing the following order:

"Headquarters First Division Fourteenth Army Corps.

"NEAR DALLAS, GA., May 28, 1864.
"COLONEL:

"Gen. Johnson desires me to express to you his high appreciation of the gallantry exhibited by the whole of your brigade in the night engagement of the 27th inst. The admirable spirit displayed by them on that occasion is above all things desirable and commendable. Soldiers animated by such courage and fortitude are capable of the very highest achievements.

"Considering the short time of your connection with this brigade as its commanding officer, the good conduct of your troops was equally creditable to you and to them. The General commanding is proud of both.

"You will publish this to each regiment of your brigade.

"Very respectfully, your obedient servant,

"E. T. WELLS, Capt. and A. A. G.

"To Col. B. F. Scribner, Com. Third Brig. First Division 14th A. C."

But this night's work was not wholly agreeable to Gen. Johnston, for when the enemy discovered that we had withdrawn from their front, they renewed the fire from their artillery with increased vigor. They doubtless felt as if they had let a bird go, and to console themselves, or to give vent to their disappointment, they continued furiously to fire at random at the wheat-field and knoll.

Johnson, Carlin and I had lain down upon the ground to get some sleep before the day dawned, when a cannon-ball came bounding along the ground and unfortunately struck Gen. Johnson in the side, and inflicted a painful though not serious injury.

For several days after the incident above related, the enemy became thoroughly aroused and made desperate and repeated efforts to find a yielding point in our lines. Johnston did not relish the impending necessity of evacuating his stronghold at Allatoona. He also wished to prevent us from extending our lines to the railroad at Ackworth, and for several days fierce battles were fought on various parts of the lines.

At length Gen. McPherson, after a desperate

battle, succeeded in relieving his command from the grip of the enemy and moved to the left. This movement was continued by other forces, until Sherman made secure his connection with his lines of supply, and thereby forced Johnston to evacuate his strong position and fall back toward the Kennesaw Mountains.

We were now undergoing another phase of warfare. The country was sparsely inhabited and was interspersed with mountains, hills and ravines, and covered with a dense forest, mostly of pine. The enemy was always found to be well protected by breastworks, and we were not long in adopting similar means of protection. We all realized that we had a wily foe in Gen. Johnston.

Early one morning Gen. Sherman was passing along my lines, and, accosting me and pointing to a house near by, said: "Do you see that house? Joe Johnston had his breakfast there this morning, and now he is gone and has not left behind even a cracker-box."

Johnston in falling back was shortening his lines and increasing his force, while we were lengthening ours and diminishing our force;

for as we progressed and gained point after point, we were forced to leave behind us detachments to protect them. In an isolated and precarious position, with an alert enemy confronting us, we were admonished to act with caution and not make any mistakes. Our intrenchments were our quarters, where the men cooked their rations and slept. There was no more regular encampment laid out, but officers and the men abode together near their places in line. There were no more formal guard mountings and dress parades. More serious and important business employed us. It was a life and death struggle, and all felt the responsibilities of the situation. Under this tremendous strain Sherman's army was subjected for an hundred days, and battles of more or less severity were fought. We were fighting by day and marching and fortifying by night. No sooner were our breastworks made secure than the retreat of the enemy made necessary changes in our position, and involved the construction of other defenses.

All the prejudice and discontent which during the first months of the war were manifested by the private soldiers toward officers, had now been dispelled. No more was heard the taunt that the officers obtained all the privileges and pay while the privates did all the fighting. They could now see the propriety and the necessity of officers, and appreciated their duties and responsibilities. All now coöperated with each other, and as they worked together in constructing their defenses, perhaps a private soldier would suggest a deflection in the line to obtain a cross-fire along a ravine, which his officer had not observed. For intelligence, tact and courage our infantry would compare favorably with any the world has produced. They would place boughs of trees in their bosoms to conceal their presence on the skirmish line. One skirmisher would ask another to draw the fire of the enemy to enable him safely to reach a rock or stump, thereby to advance or improve the line. There was no discontent, no complaining, no insubordination, but all dwelt together like a large family with the father and elder brothers to respect and love. They were as one man, united and determined to conquer! While they properly appreciated the skill of the leaders of the enemy, their confidence in the ability of their own Chief was unbounded. Gen. Sherman was designated by them as "The Old Man," or "Uncle Billie," and Gen. Thomas they affectionately called "Pap."

The men had now outlived the foolish disposition to depreciate the Eastern troops. The sobriquet, "Fighting Joe Hooker," had been modified by them to "Pugnacious Joe," and for short they used the diminutive "P. J." They would ridicule the paper collars worn by Hooker's men by buttoning one on their coats so as to have one end of the collar hang down on their breast, as if they did not know how to wear them. But after the battles of Wauhatchie, Lookout Mountain and Resaca all this feeling disappeared. An officer said to me during the fight at Resaca, "I take it all back that I have insinuated about 'P. J.,' for I notice in our counsels of war that when he urges an assault upon the enemy, he is always willing to make it himself. He don't want the right to make the charge because he is on the left, but, on the contrary, is always ready and willing to fight." When Hooker was on my flank I felt sure that he was on the lookout to coöperate should the chance occur, and had he been on Griffin's flank when some weeks later the Thirty-eighth carried the rebel works at Jonesboro, Hardee's corps would in all probability have been captured.

The low estimate with which the regular army officers regarded the volunteers, during the early stages of the war, was also now changed. Then they were impatient, irritable and abusive, and if profanity was included in the course of study at West Point, I am sure that the Army of the Cumberland had their share of the prize scholars in this branch. One day while at Green River, a young Lieutenant of mine was deluged by a shower of words such as the Christian Commission does not use; but he continued to smile blandly as the torrent fell, and this increasing the irritation of his assailant, and "What are you laughing at?" being furiously demanded (I omit the lurid adjective and thereby shorten the question), the Lieutenant, with his face wreathed in smiles, replied, "Well, I expect to be a brigadier-general myself before this war is over, and it makes me laugh to think how fast I am learning how to behave."

I have been incensed to have large details, to work upon the fortifications and bridge, report at six o'clock in the morning, as ordered, and then have to wait in the mud and weather until nine o'clock for His High Mightiness to rise from his slumber and eat his breakfast before the necessary orders could be given. The West Point education these officers had received, however useful and superior, did not supply that experience in war which both regular and volunteer had yet to acquire. I will frankly add that after these regular army officers had achieved something to be proud of, they became considerate of the feelings of others, and in every way worthy of the splendid educations they had received. I served during the war in the same division with a regular brigade, and was indebted to many of the officers for information and explanations, which were needed, as from time to time my studies were pursued. Gen. King and Major Ely were especially kind to me, and one would have to seek long before more unostentatious and courteous gentlemen could be found. During the early days of my service I was perplexed at receiving an order to detail two hundred men to report at headquarters with a large number of picks and shovels and axes. Had the earth been demanded I would have been as able to respond to it as I was to fill the requisition for the required implements. In my dilemma I consulted Gen. King, whose advice at once relieved my anxiety. He said, just take the blank form and make a requisition upon the division quartermaster for the implements called for, which in all probability he will not have on hand, but have him indorse that fact upon the paper, and you will thus have something to show if any explanations are needed for your failure to obey the order. In matters like this and concerning boards of survey, I was kindly assisted to understand the army regulations by friends among the regular brigade.

I happened one day to be at division headquarters when a young officer who had been sent for appeared. The General was very angry and reprimanded him very severely. It seems that the officer had been on guard duty and had detained a courier with dispatches all night outside the guard lines. He stated in his defense that the orders he had received from the officer he had relieved, were, that in the daytime he was to permit no one to pass in or out without a pass signed by the General commanding, and that at night he was to pass no one without the countersign. "And this courier had neither pass nor countersign, and I could not, under my orders, permit him to pass." The General referred him to the army regulations, which described the duty of the pickets in such cases; but the officer had not advanced that far with his military education. The General let him off, but admonished him in a way that made a profound impression upon me, and was of lasting service. He said, "Words at best very imperfectly express the thoughts of the mind; orders are addressed to intelligent beings and not to wooden men; ordinary common sense is always presumed, and they must be read and interpreted in the light of reason. Orders must be construed and obeyed in this light, and you must be willing to risk your honor and your life upon the correctness of your judgment and obedience."

Thus, day by day, experience brought us knowledge. Among the practical results of this acquired knowledge was a change in the knapsacks. This subject had for years puzzled the authorities at Washington. The difficulty was to provide something in which the men could carry their necessary belongings that would not cut and chafe their shoulders and chests, and yet could be quickly put on and taken off. This problem proved difficult to solve by the quartermaster department, but the men had now settled the question themselves. By putting their change of raiment on their blankets, the gum one on the outside, and rolling all up together lengthwise, and then tying the ends together, forming a loop, which they could throw over one shoulder and under the other, as the scarf is worn by our officer of the day, the thing was done. It thus formed a cushion for the gun, could be easily shifted from one shoulder to the other, and could be quickly put off when they halted on the march to rest. A knife and fork and a tin plate in the haversack, a frying pan and tin cup outside suspended from it, and the soldier had all the cooking utensils and tableware he needed! Only one wagon was allowed to a brigade. Buell and Rosecrans specified what the soldier should have with him, and limited the officers in the size and weight of their baggage. But Sherman did not meddle in such matters, and no restraint whatever was placed by him as to what they should have, but they were allowed to take anything they could carry upon their persons. Therefore, upon this campaign, the wardrobes of the officers were not very extensive or elaborate. One was often reminded of the man who, having but one shirt, buttoned up his coat to conceal its absence when in the wash, and upon being interrogated upon the scantiness of his wardrobe replied, "Would you have me have a thousand?" Many of my officers were reduced to this extremity and to the necessity of washing their own underwear in the creek, remaining in the water for a bath while their clothes were drying on the bushes. One day a party of them were thus situated when the batteries of the enemy were opened, and shot and shell began to fall in alarming proximity to the bathers, who, for safety, were forced in unmade toilets to flee to the breastworks amidst the jeers and ridicule of the troops in line. Upton's tactics is another result of experience. The commands in battle of the old tactics were very complicated and impracticable. Upton's wheeling by fours to march by the flank is so much simpler than the doubling and undoubling that the matter need only be referred to here.

That order of Gen. Buell prohibiting moving by the flank when on the march, and prescribing instead section and platoon formation, was very absurd when the narrow and obstructed roads are considered. The passage of lines is another incongruity. I never saw it done on the field as laid down in the books. The objective point in tactics seems to me to be the making them conform to what men will without forethought do in the emergencies of battle. A good illustration of the effect of drill and discipline upon the intuitive and automatic actions of men, occurred at Stone River. Before the Thirty-eighth emerged from the cedars on the first day's fight, they were formed in line left in front, and after they were dispersed to more safely cross the open field, they reformed on the pike left in front in the same order as they were in the cedars. In a conversation with that model soldier, Gen. Sheridan, just after his return from Europe, where he witnessed some of the battles of the Franco-German war, the descriptions of the battles of Frederick the Great were referred to, and the General was asked if the movements on the field were performed in that manner. He answered that they performed their evolutions and advanced in line very much as we did.

Old soldiers when overpowered or taken at a disadvantage may yield ground; but they will keep together as if attracted to each other by a sort of moral gravitation, and will halt when beyond the missiles of the enemy. On the contrary, when raw troops become panic-stricken they cannot be rallied within the noise of battle. Not having acquired that cohesion which long association and discipline give, they will so disperse that much time and effort must be employed to collect them for further duty. But old soldiers will unconsciously reform their ranks, even as the cavalry horses are said to have done when abandoned by their riders, who had embarked in ships on which the horses could not be taken. These old war steeds thus turned loose upon the coast did but exercise the habits acquired by drill and discipline, when they formed themselves into squadrons and charged upon and destroyed each other. The behavior of the old soldiers at Stone River, Chickamauga and Bentonville illustrates these differences, and contrasts with the conduct of the raw troops at Richmond, Ky., Perryville, and other battles during the first year of the war.

In order to realize the rapidity and facility with which the men constructed their fortifications, let the reader imagine himself a brigade commander. You are approaching the halting-place when an order is brought to you to form, say on the left of Baird and right of Carlin, each regiment to fortify and picket its own front. You will send a staff officer to conduct the command to its position in the line and repeat the orders. Another officer will select the place for headquarters, and orderlies will be sent to find the wagon and direct it to the place selected. You have dismounted and are resting while supper is being prepared. After you have refreshed yourself the horses will be ordered, you will ride down the line and will find them already well protected by breastworks. To understand how so much work could be accomplished in so short a time, you must consider the great number of men that were employed. When one pine-tree has been felled, hundreds have fallen, the tops are cut off, and the log is borne to its place in the line;

another soon follows and is laid by its side; another is placed on top, the boughs are strewn along the outside, and the diggers throw up the earth to augment the power of resistance. Now, while this is being done with the three logs, the same is being done simultaneously with hundreds, and thus miles of these defenses are constructed. The top logs which were afterward added to the three here described was an invention of the enemy; but as no patent or caveat had been issued by proper authority, we did not hesitate to adopt it. This improvement was made by placing a sapling at intervals along the line with one end on the top log and the other on the ground some eight or ten feet to the rear, and on these place another log so as to leave a space between the upper logs through which the musket could be protruded in firing, and thereby the head of the soldier would be protected, and should this top log happen to be struck by a cannon-ball, it would roll down on the sapling to the rear, and would not crush the men behind the work.

The delays and difficulties to be overcome in moving a large army even a short distance in such a country with a vigilant enemy lying in wait to pounce upon us at inopportune times cannot be appreciated unless all the conditions are considered. To break a long line into columns in order to march upon such roads as had to be used, consumes much time. The same may be said of deploying the column into lines again. A small and aggressive rear guard may greatly retard and add to the difficulties and labor of such movement, for we could not prudently risk being caught unawares by the enemy in force and in fortified positions; therefore we had to be cautious and at all times ready for any contingency that might arise. All these cares and responsibilities weighed heavily upon our commanding general. And all, to a greater or less degree, shared them with him.

To add to the discomfort of our situation, a rainy season had commenced, and it rained every day for many days. But the hardships to be endured by the weather the enemy also had to bear. One day after a rain-storm we shelled the woods from which we had been harassed by sharpshooters. They were surprised by the position of our battery, and for safety were forced to seek the shelter of their rifle-pits, which were now overflowed with water. After the artillery ceased to fire, our skirmish line was rapidly pushed into the woods, and soon fifteen prisoners were captured. As they passed to the rear they resembled drowned rats more than aggressive foes. The enemy reinforced these men too late to save them. Vigorous but ineffectual efforts were made to regain the position. One of the prisoners as he approached us was observed to dodge a random missile which came whizzing by him, and he was asked by an officer, "What are you dodging for? they are your own bullets." To which he replied, "I have found out, General, that lead and iron are no respecters of persons."

As we drew near Kenesaw Mountain the country became rougher, and days passed without the sight of a habitation. One evening, however, my lines included a house within them, which I found deserted, and took possession of it for brigade headquarters. It was built of logs, had one story and several apartments, which contained some rude and clumsy looms; great quantities of woolen yarns were hung up, or stowed away in large chests which were crowded into some of the rooms. The next day the owners appeared — an old woman and a younger one, her daughter — claiming the property, and proceeded to search among the drawers and chests. They did not seem to find what they wanted, and offers of assistance were made by us, which were accepted. They sought some articles of the daughter's wardrobe, a pair of English walking shoes, a hat and a gown, which they said were done up together in a bundle, but nowhere could they be found. We all joined in the search, and as the task became more and more hopeless the anxiety and fretfulness of the daughter increased, and the elegance and costliness of the articles lost were dilated upon. The hat was imported from France, and cost seventy-five dollars in Charleston, and the shoes and the gown cost a fabulous sum. I was not a little worried at not being able to find them. They seemed to look with suspicion upon us; not that we were wearing them, but that we had taken them to present to our lady friends at home. At last, after ransacking every hole and corner about the premises, a bundle was discovered, and I knew by the start of recognition, made by the women, that the treasures were found. They hastily opened the bundle, and the gorgeous apparel proved to be an old shabby dress, a pair of shoes run down at the heel, and a bonnet that was by no means "nobby." I will venture to assert that had they not been surprised into identifying the bundle they would have disowned it and ignored the contents as their belongings. From this and other experiences I am led to believe that the government has paid out vast sums for losses which had been thus overvalued.

CHAPTER XI.

A BATTLE IN A THUNDER-STORM.

ON the 18th of June the Fourteenth Corps advanced to an extended ridge in front of which lay open fields. The extent and form of these fields were defined by the dense forest which surrounded them. In front of our division the trees grew much nearer to us than to other parts of the line. The ground sloped away from us toward a stream which was indicated by bushes lining its banks. Near this point the enemy was supposed to be in force, and to assault them we were now in line.

The morning was cloudy and threatened us with our daily rations of rain; some delay was made in the vain hope that the sky would clear, but Gen. Palmer announced that there would be no postponement on account of weather. He did this, I think, contrary to his judgment, for he said that Sherman had complained to

Thomas that some of the troops hugged their entrenchments too closely, and, although we now had none before us, he was unwilling that Sherman should think that we shrank from the rain; so the line advanced. The way of the right of my command lay through the woods, while my left was exposed in the open ground. Our artillery commenced the fight and was promptly responded to by the guns of the enemy. But how shall I describe the conflict in which both nature and man were combined to appall and destroy? The foreboded storm had burst upon us. The thunder pealed, and the forked lightning flashed in fitful gleams, and glared in the blackened sky. Now the rattle of musketry joined in the grand and awful symphony, and now the floodgates were opened, and the rain poured down. Solid shot and explosive shells fell among the overhanging branches of the trees, and, crackling and crashing, the limbs fell about us, made more visible by the bursting shells and flashes from the angry sky. Every note in the scale was audible from treble to bass as from a mighty organ. The caliber of each gun sent forth its missiles with its proper note; the rifle and musket ball carried the air, while the accompanying bass rumbled and groaned from the thunder above and artilery below, which shook the earth and reverberated in the heavens. Throughout this detonating din and roar ran the theme as in a grand and soul-stirring opera. Staff officers dashed to and fro with orders concerning the movement, and as they were orally delivered, the officers would lift their feet from their stirrups to permit the water which overflowed their top-boots to pour from them. Amid all the clangor and uproar the business in hand was not lost sight of. When we reached the stream which we expected to find at the foot of the slope, we could see the entrenchments of the enemy, which could only be approached by us over the open space in their front. While my division commander and I were consulting together Capt. Dilger rode up. His battery had been assigned to my command. He pointed out a spot where he wished to take his battery. I objected, and said to him that the place was not in our front, and that Gen. Baird, in whose front it was, should use one of his own batteries there, if he thought it desirable. He replied, "I ask it as a favor, for Gen. Baird wanted some guns placed there, and his chief of artillery persuaded him from it, saying that a battery could not live a minute in such a place." The Captain was so earnest that I looked inquiringly to the General, who answered me aside, "Let him do it," and soon the six guns, drawn by twenty-four horses, came clattering and splashing down, and, sweeping out into the open space in front of the works of the enemy, they were unlimbered, and the horses rapidly sent to the rear for protection, while the guns were loaded and fired with a rapidity I have never seen excelled. The men went to work to construct defenses for the guns. I intended to make a detail for this purpose, but Dilger was a great favorite with the men, and volunteers in abundance soon came forward for the work. The Captain was known by them as "Leather-breeches," and was rarely spoken of by any other name or title. When cover for a gun had been sufficiently completed to afford protection to it, it was moved by hand to its place. Their fire did not cease or slacken, but was kept up continuously and vigorously under the galling fire of the enemy, who had concentrated his batteries upon them. The rebel infantry also soon joined in the combat, and soon the battle raged along the line, and did not abate until darkness enshrouded the scene. Next day the enemy abandoned their works, and fell back to their stronghold at Kenesaw Mountain.

On the night of the 20th I relieved Gen. Harker. It was very dark and the ground was soaked with rain. As the General conducted me along the trenches we often had to wade in the semi-fluid mud. The moist sides of the ditches that we rubbed against, as we passed through them, so covered us with the wet clay that the blue of our uniforms was changed to the butternut worn by many of the rebels. While Harker was showing me the defenses he expressed his inability to explain some of the intricacies of the labyrinths, but assured me that I would soon find out their usefulness. Gen. Whittaker had gallantly carried the position, but the rebels seemed discontented and were loath to give it up, and made frequent but ineffectual efforts to regain it. The enemy must have had their suspicions aroused by the noises unconsciously made by the troops in making the change, for, before daylight, they concentrated their artillery upon us. We held the position for two days, subjected to frequent terriffc bombardments. I verified Harker's prediction and found out the reason for the zigzag traverses, and we were very willing to avail ourselves of the protection they afforded. Here Capt. Dilger again proved himself equal to the occasion, and handled his guns with admirable skill.

Before daylight on the 23d we relieved Gen. Kimball at Bald Knob. This point had also been carried only after a brave struggle. But the enemy became desperate and afterward succeeded in retaking it, but had to yield it again to us. Kenesaw Mountain now rose boldly a short distance to our left and front, and Johnston's main line was not more than three hundred yards in front of ours. This proximity to them the rebels could not abide, and Bald Knob was the bone of contention as long as they remained near it.

Reference has been made to many changes of opinion and practice among the troops brought about by experience, but none were more marked than the free and open ways they availed themselves of shelter from bullets and cannon-balls.

During the earlier periods of the war they would have felt themselves disgraced if discovered behind a tree or log for protection, and I confess that I shared with them much of this feeling. In the cedars at Stone River Gen. Rousseau sent a staff officer several times to urge me to dismount from my horse, which I indignantly refused to do, and argued, but not very logically, that a colonel was a mounted officer and should be willing to take the risk involved in his rank and position on the field, and should he dismount in action, he would be taking the chances of some other man and might be killed. Therefore I preferred to take the risks of my own proper position in the line of duty. There is, however, this much truth in my reasoning: there is no safe place in a battle. As many men are killed in the rear rank as the front rank. At Resaca two men skulked on the side of a hill in the rear of the battle-field and were both killed by random bullets. When the rounds of ammunition expended in a fight are compared with the number of killed and wounded, the great excess of random shots is appreciated. If, however, the close grazes, the misses by a hair-breadth, could be added to the effective shots, the number of random bullets would be greatly reduced. The question has been asked, "What becomes of all the pins?" The inquiry could as properly be made, "What becomes of all the bullets?" From these considerations the assertion may be ventured that the safest place in a battle is where it is a duty to be.

But of all the miserable and unhappy places for a soldier to be while a battle is raging, is among the wagon trains in the rear. Here the stragglers collect to palliate their cowardice; and, to mitigate the contempt they are conscious of deserving, they proceed to magnify the dangers and destruction at the front, and to invent disasters that have overtaken the army. Thus the shirks are kept in a continual turmoil of fear and anxiety.

Without undervaluing the importance of skillful generalship and a knowledge of the art of war which should be displayed in the conduct of a battle, yet the best strategy is to fight. Victory is often achieved by the troops that hold out even for a moment after both sides have become impressed with the idea that they will all be killed and must fly for safety. Gen. Grant, when, as colonel, he first moved on the enemy in Missouri, was consoled with the reflection that the rebel soldiers were as badly scared as his were.

An officer commits a grave mistake when he permits his men to withdraw from a combat because they are vigorously assaulted, and casualties occurring. Only special and imperative reasons can justify it. The men will be led to expect the same thing on other occasions, and will never know when you really mean business. They should be taught to depend upon success alone for victory, for safety and for rest.

A young backwoodsman of the Thirty-eighth expressed the gist of what I mean. On the night of the battle of Lookout Mountain, Col. Griffin had his men throw up breastworks of stones. "Coon," as he was dubbed by the men, objected to so much hard work, and drawled out in his broad country dialect, "I thought a feller had to take some risks when he went to war?" Coon may not have been graceful or stylish, but he did not lack sense.

A soldier's many risks and narrow escapes, I

think, tend to promote that belief in fatalism so generally ascribed to him, which enables him to more clearly see the humor of Gonzalo in Shakespeare's "Tempest," who says: "I have great comfort from this fellow; methinks he hath no drowning marks upon him; his complexion is perfect gallows. Stand fast, good fate, to his hanging; make the rope of his destiny our cable, for our own doth little advantage! If he is not born to be hanged, our case is most miserable." Now, while I have never heard of a good soldier hanging, I have known them to reason like Gonzalo.

No characteristic of an officer is more respected by the men than courage. Having this, other good traits are presupposed. He may be irritable, overbearing, partial to favorites, rash, and may lead them into unnecessary peril and slaughter; but if he shows pluck and shares the danger with them, they will sooner or later forgive him everything. They may criticise him among themselves, but they will not permit outsiders to do so. On the other hand, an officer may possess all the virtues of the human character, but if he once show the white feather his influence and usefulness is ended. A soldier during the battle of Chickamauga fell into disgrace among his comrades by lack of pluck, either real or supposed. This so weighed upon his mind and so filled him with mortification, that on Lookout Mountain, during the night fight, he climbed up on a rock where the shots were rushing by as if poured from a sieve, and called out, " Now, any of you that think I am a coward and thinks himself braver than I am, just come up here!" But the words were hardly uttered when he fell, pierced by many bullets. This feeling in a great measure explains the popularity of Gen. Rousseau with the troops. When he showed himself on the battle-field with his hat raised on the point of his sword, encouraging or urging them into the fight, his influence over them was unbounded. He was their Murat, their Ajax, and at all times, in season and out of season, they recognized him with cheers. So frequent were these manifestations, that any unusual stir in the camp would be ascribed "either to Rousseau or a rabbit." Other attributes doubtless added to this favor he found with the men. His fine physique, noble bearing, his thoroughbred horse and gorgeous trappings caught their eyes and aroused their enthusiasm. With all this splendor he was without ostentation, and he was easily approached. His frank and genial expression seemed to invite the hurrahs of the troops when he appeared among them.

Rousseau was deficient in technical knowledge on military subjects, and if by reading the tactics and army regulations once over he could have been assured that ever afterward he would know their contents, it is very doubtful whether he would have taken so much pains. But the men thought he knew it all. He would not even study his maps, and often turned them over to me unopened. And yet when Rousseau came upon the battle-field, he had that *coup d'œil*, that intuitive comprehension, that broad and far-reaching common sense, that boldness and determination, which carried every one away with him and secured success.

Here let me give a word of caution and advice to the young soldier of the future. Should you have the choosing of the officers who are to command you, do not select an easy-going, kind-hearted, clever fellow in preference to a careful, just and efficient one. A soldier who means to do his duty is protected by good discipline, while the shirk goes free under lax and uncertain rules. Great injustice was done me from the inconsiderate "luck-and-go-easy" disposition of Gen. Rousseau. At Stone River he was very demonstrative in his approval of my conduct, and frequently sent me words of praise during the battle. He addressed me with affectionate and complimentary diminutives. He placed my hand over his heart and invoked blessings on my head. Yet in his official report he only mentioned my name in a general way. He went home after the battle, and wrote his report in the intervals between the parties and banquets given him by his admiring friends, and in the language of his chief of staff, "He neither did justice to himself nor to his command."

When he returned to his division and found my name left out in the lists for promotion, he manifested so much chagrin and made such effort to repair the injury done me, that I could not help forgiving him. He petitioned the President in my behalf, and obtained the indorsement thereon of the name of every division commander of the Army of the Cumberland, and those of the corps commanders. This was favorably indorsed and forwarded to Mr. Lincoln by the commanding general. He also instigated Gen. Thomas to make a supplementary report of the battle, which was concurred in and forwarded to the secretary of war by Gen. Rosecrans (see report of Stone River, page 55). But all this was of no avail; the victory of Stone River had become an old song, and the quantum of promotions had been made.

Gen. Rousseau was large-hearted, brave and generous, and from our meetings during the Mexican war to the day of his death we were always good friends.

In the management of men it is of the utmost importance to maintain their *amour propre*. Nearly every one fixes some standard, draws a line somewhere, within which he intends to stay. One is ambitious to have his gun in the stack at the close of each day's march; another prides himself on never failing to be ready for duty when his turn for detail comes; another wishes to be able to boast that he never was arrested, or in the guard-house; and still another takes pride in the fact that he never was drunk;—and so each man has some point of honor which he desires to maintain. But, once these resolves are broken, they are apt to take seven devils worse than the first. The officer is fortunate who can discern the points of difference in the dispositions of his men, not only for their good, but also for the good of the service. It is a mistake to govern too much, to issue orders that cannot be enforced, or to carry discipline beyond that proper self-respect and manliness which a good soldier always possesses.

In order to bring out some interesting traits of character, I will take for a text Joe Redding, of the Thirty-eighth. He was first sergeant of Company D at the commencement of the service of the regiment. Unfortunately, he encountered the displeasure of Lieut.-Col. Merriweather, who was in command of the regiment while I was on duty at Nashville. Joe's trouble resulted in his reduction to the ranks. This was regretted by me, for Joe was a good sergeant, and I saw in him elements of efficiency. To the surprise of many, he was not demoralized by his disgrace, but was as good a private soldier as he had been a sergeant. In him was manifest that distinction which exists between fortitude and courage, both of which qualities he possessed in a high degree. No hardship or privation could make him complain. He could bear with composure, and even dignity, hunger, thirst, cold and fatigue, which so often oppress and chafe even the most courageous men. He possessed an independent, manly spirit, and had withal a certain grim humor that made him a favorite with his friends. After dress-parade one Saturday evening at Battle Creek, when the officers marched up in line to salute, I detained them to say that the Sunday morning inspection would be made on the parade ground, and that I had invited Gen. Sill to be present, and added that I was sure that nothing more need be said to insure a creditable turn-out. The officers made this known to the men, and soon all were busy furbishing up their arms and accouterments. It is told of Joe that he was alone in his tent, and while engaged in polishing his gun, he thus soliloquised, "We are going to have a grand inspection to-morrow morning. Gen. Sill is coming to it. The General will point me out to the Colonel and ask him, 'Who is that fine, soldierly looking fellow?' The Colonel will reply, 'That is Joe Redding; once an orderly sergeant, but now reduced to the ranks.' The General will exclaim, 'Why, he ought to be an officer!'"

Joe was taken prisoner at Chickamauga and had an eventful time. He made his escape and had almost reached the Union lines at Knoxville, when he was retaken. He afterward tried it again and succeeded. While he was a prisoner no abuse or threats could subdue him or dampen his spirit, silence his aggressive tongue, or stop his patriotic songs. The pain of the inquisition could not have made him wilt or truckle. On the Atlanta campaign he had been made a lieutenant. At Jonesboro, when the Thirty-eighth had made their way through the abattis in front of the enemy's fortifications, the color-bearer was killed, his bleeding body falling forward upon the flag against the reverse side of the rebel embankment. Here the regiment for an instant seemed to linger for shelter from the deadly fire that was poured into them. They seemed to hesitate to climb over the works before the rebels recovered from the surprise and shock of the charge upon them. At a critical moment Joe rolled the dead body of the color-bearer from the blood-stained flag, and, snatching it up and mounting the works, he threw the flag toward the enemy, exclaiming to the men, "Boys, there it goes!" and, leaping after it, was followed by the regiment. Again seizing the flag, Joe bore it victoriously throughout the day.

I remember in my youth reading a story told of a combat between the Scotch and the Saracens. When all seemed lost to the Scotch the brave Douglass in command took from his plaid a golden ball, and flinging it amidst the Saracens cried out, "There goes the heart of Bruce!" Then all the Scotch rushed after it, and the day was gained. Now I fail to discover any essential difference in the heroism displayed by the gallant Redding.

CHAPTER XII.

THE BEGINNING OF THE END.

DURING our stay at Bald Knob, artillery duels were of frequent occurrence. The enemy had several batteries in position which had the range of our works, and at times opened them all upon us. On the summit of the mountain they had heavy siege guns, like those they used on Lookout Mountain. It was gratifying as well as surprising to find so little damage following one of these terrific bombardments. Solid shot and shell from different directions would strike our works or fall within our lines, tearing up the earth and scattering dangerous missiles in all directions, or they would rush screaming over our heads in a manner that would have appalled the bravest heart a few months before. But the men had now become familiar with such demonstrations, and were no longer disconcerted by them. After their uproar subsided, some waggish soldier would crawl out from his cover, and with extravagant gesticulation and bombast cry out in imitation of an official bulletin, "One killed and two wounded," or in other ways ridicule the effort.

The ground in the rear of our lines sloped back from the curved crest of the hill to the woods below, forming a cup-shaped space, over which the men had to pass in going to and fro from their quarters in the trenches to the rear for water or provisions. Into this cup or pot, as the men named it, great quantities of shells exploded, rendering the passage over it very dangerous while the cannonading was going on. The men, therefore, had either to run the gauntlet or wait for a lull in the storm. A soldier assigned as a reason for calling it a pot, "The rebels threw their pot-metal there." Another suggested that it would be a good place for a junk shop, there was so much old iron lying about.

One day a surgeon who had been detailed in the general hospital at Nashville was returning to his regiment, and crossing the pot just when the shells began to fall and explode. The doctor wore a long linen duster, which, like a plug hat or raised umbrella, was of itself sufficient to draw the attention of the men to him; but when he, terror-stricken and frantic, rushed toward the breastworks for protection with the skirts of his duster fluttering in the breeze, there were a thousand voices yelling out the greeting, "How are you, sanitary commission?"

The acute sense of the ludicrous and the latent or developed humor and wit of the American can nowhere be more strikingly observed than among the soldiers. One may be attired and coached by a Lord Chesterfield, without spot or wrinkle; he may be unconscious of any defect in his appointments and bearing; yet the Argus eye of the soldier will not fail to perceive some weak place, some vulnerable heel, not touched by the protecting care. An incident somewhat illustrative of this occurred a short time before my assignment to the Third Brigade, and made quite a stir in the First Brigade at the time. The story has been often related, and versions of it have been published in the newspapers in various parts of the country. It is known as "The Dog Story." I will tell it from my own standpoint.

One day an orderly from division headquarters brought me a communication which stated that marauding parties were abroad in the land killing sheep and hogs, and pillaging from the inhabitants in the neighborhood everything edible they could lay hands on. I was instructed to station pickets on the various roads leading into camp, and to arrest all persons returning to it with booty. The provisions were to be seized and turned over to the commissary department. My mortification was great to receive such charges and orders, for like the swan who thinks her own the whitest, my men were thought to be above such conduct, and the accusations were deemed to be but an overdrawn picture of overzealous scouts. At that time there was no scarcity of rations, and therefore no excuse for foraging. Nevertheless the pickets were placed, and soon, to my surprise and chagrin, the foragers began to return ladened with pork, veal and mutton, all of which was duly turned over to the brigade commissary. The culprits in charge of the provost guard were taken to the division commander for his action. What this was I do not now remember, but they were soon after returned to duty. They were not, however, all of them from my command, and the confiscated meat was afterward issued to the provost guard and the enlisted men at brigade headquarters, as there was about sufficient for a ration for them, but not enough for the regiments, and thus the matter was disposed of and dismissed from further attention.

But soon signs of disorder began to prevail in the camp, and Capt. De Bruin, the provost marshal, and his guards were to be seen rushing to and fro chasing fugitives, who with the aid of their comrades succeeded in escaping. It was soon currently reported, and believed by the men, that a party interested in the provisions seized had passed out of the lines, and having killed and dressed a large fat dog, had returned with portions of its carcass and managed to have it confiscated and placed with the meat already taken. And now when one or more of the provost guards were observed by the men in suitable localities, they were assailed with all the caressing, flattering, coaxing terms that are applied to a favorite dog. This would enrage the Captain and his men, and produced the confusion. To such an extent did this prevail, that I was forced to issue a circular to regimental commanders. Their attention was directed to the arduous and important duties which devolved upon the provost marshal, and the demoralizing tendency of such disrespect to his authority, and urged them to coöperate in maintaining order. They did all they could to suppress the disorder, but without complete success. At night, or from the midst of a lot of men, would issue whistling and dog calls, which so provoked and harrassed the provost marshal and his men that their lives became a burden. At last I sent for the Captain and assured him that everything would be done that could be done to maintain his dignity and authority, but that the men thought they had played a good trick upon him, and that they would have their fun though the sky fell, and that the secretary of war or President of the United States had not the power to stop a soldier from enjoying his joke, and that as long as they saw his irritation they would keep it up, and that the joke would cling to him until he ignored the whole matter and ceased to pay any attention whatever to it. He took my advice and the subject was soon dropped, for the Captain was a good officer, and the men at heart liked him. But the soldier is no respecter of persons when such humors seize him.

A novel reason assigned for a furlough affords another illustration of a soldier's humor. When the mustering officer was expected at our camp of rendezvous, all recruiting parties were called in. Many of the company officers went in person after their absent men. One of the captains was hurrying to camp with a wagon-load of men, and passing one of his recruits on the road, urged him to jump in forthwith, at the same time assuring him that after the muster he could return and bid good-bye to his family. So in to the wagon he crowded, and was thus brought to camp. But after the muster we were ordered off to join Sherman, to forestall, if possible, Buckner's entry into Louisville. Now, after several months' service this man applied for a furlough, which at that time was especially difficult to obtain. He urged his suit with pertinacity, referring to the above circumstances, and thus closed his appeal, "I left my oxen right in the road chained to a saw-log; now, Colonel, them steers ought to be unhitched and fed."

THE BEGINNING OF THE END. 291

Between my lines and the troops on the right a road had been made, over which the artillery horses were taken to the creek for water. We were often amused by the antics of a soldier who had evidently been a circus-actor previous to his enlistment. He would stand upon the back of his horse and attitudinize as he passed up the slope, as only a professional rider could do. It is very doubtful whether he ever had so large an audience, or been so wildly applauded, as he was here.

The varied occupations of the men before they became soldiers, was often a source of wonder. Frequent orders were received from headquarters detailing bridge builders, carpenters, blacksmiths, machinists, upholsterers, millers, telegraphers, engineers and pilots. The demands for the last two, to serve on the gun-boats, took some of my best men. This versatility of knowledge in the Union army was an important factor in the success that crowned their efforts. While at Kenesaw the bridge over the Etowah was destroyed, and the railroad in our rear torn up. It is said that while a rebel adjutant was reading a congratulatory order to the troops, which enumerated the disasters that would overtake us in consequence thereof, the whistle of our locomotive was heard by them, which announced that the damage was already repaired.

Orders were frequently received to open out with the battery at a specified hour, which I suppose was to cover some movement, or to make the rebels show themselves, and thereby prove to us that they were yet in our front, or not, as usual, falling back. One morning, just as Dilger had commenced to fire, in compliance with one of these orders, the enemy replied with unexpected readiness and vigor from sixteen guns. It soon became a serious matter to us. They had our range and used their guns with terrible effect. Our battery was planted on our front line with the infantry on the right and left of it. This point of the knob was a salient, and had a range to the left toward the mountain, also one to the front and an oblique one to the right of us. Of course, the enemy, by placing guns at certain points, could converge on us, and this they did with much precision, and we were very well satisfied when they slackened and then ceased firing. This was the first time they had succeeded in projecting a ball through one of our embrasures. Dilger frequently did so to theirs. But now they had dismounted one of our guns, had killed one of the Captain's best sergeants, besides other casualties. His fortifications were so battered that they could have been shaken down with the hand, and one more direct hit would have made a breach. The Captain, in reporting to me the situation, said in his foreign dialect, "The enemy deceive me; I contract for smooth bores, they give me rifles; they change guns on me; they deceive me!"

Soon, as many men as could work without attracting attention to the dilapidated condition of the place, were employed in repairing the damages. At night, to make sure against another similar attack the next day, I had rifle-pits dug well out in the field in front of the rebel batteries, and these were occupied by sharpshooters who had a good range. Care was taken to have them near enough to our works to enable them to reach shelter before a sortie of the enemy could overtake and capture them. The next morning when the enemy uncovered his embrasures, our bullets would enter them with such rapidity and precision that the battery was silenced and would be silenced as often as they attempted to use it. Capt. Dilger was amazed at the efficiency of this means, and, pointing to the rifle-pits, remarked, "Just so good as a battery!"

Artillery men are very sensitive to musket-balls. Cannon against cannon they appear to delight in; they seem to feel complimented when the enemy turns his guns upon them; but a musket-ball they despise, and when they begin to hiss about them or to strike their guns with a sound like a spat or splash, they begin to grumble, and think they are not properly supported.

Capt. Dilger came to me one day for permission to take two of his guns out from their defenses into the field in front of the troops on our right. He added that Gen. Wood wished him to do so. I forbade it, and this time he did not insist; but after a pause he resumed, saying, "I am glad not to go there, for I would lose some horses, and I am very scarce of horses." He did not seem to consider that he would also lose some men.

The last time I ever met this gallant and

efficient officer was when I called on him one day to give him some directions. It rained, as usual, that day, and had not ceased. The guns were covered in the tarpaulins, under which the company had crawled for shelter. I called out and was promptly answered by the Captain. As he emerged bare-headed into the weather I besought him to remain where he was; that I could say to him what I had to say just as well there. But he persisted in coming out, and standing forth he saluted and said, "I cannot remain under cover while my officer stands in the rain giving me orders." The recollection of this noble soldier, with his manly bearing and graceful form, will never be effaced from my memory. He bore a large red scar upon his cheek. I know not how or when it was received, but I venture the assertion that it blushed from no dishonor.

The cordial and frequent intercourse with my officers when in command of the First Brigade, did not obtain with the Third, for on this campaign the conditions were very unfavorable to social or even official contact, and communications were chiefly maintained through staff-officers. There were no drills or parades to throw the officers together. The forests, ravines and breastworks in which they lived and fought, so obscured them and shut them off from each other, that only those whose positions in the line were contiguous, could conveniently meet each other. The Third Brigade was also unfortunate in losing by killed and wounded four regimental commanders. In addition to those already mentioned is Lieut.-Col. Ward, of the Thirty-seventh Indiana. He was shot in the face at New Hope Church. When I saw him with bloody countenance passing to the rear, I felt that startle of surprise that always attends the loss of a friend. While we may be sure that such losses will occur in a battle, one is never prepared for the loss of a particular person.

Col. Neibling, of the Twenty-first Ohio, was in delicate health. It was thought that he was far gone in consumption, but when he lost his arm it is said that his health was restored, and his lungs were healed during the suppuration of his wound. The last time I met Gen. Sherman on this campaign was near the Chattahoochee River. My brigade was in reserve, and the regular brigade was engaged at the front. It had been intimated that the Third Brigade was to relieve them that night, so I rode forward to examine the situation. I found the brigade in a brisk little fight, and to my surprise and alarm I discovered Gen. Sherman in a field in the rear of the combat. He was subjected to much danger from random bullets and from sharpshooters. I rode up to him and expressed my concern for his safety, and protested against his thus exposing himself, and added, "What would become of us should anything happen to you?" He curtly replied, "What are you doing here?" I answered by explaining as above.

One day, while near Kingston, I was over at headquarters of Gen. Thomas. His tents were pitched on three sides of a parallelogram in a field covered with grass. Standing in front of one of the tents in conversation with Gens. Elliott and Newton, I was surprised at being accosted by Gen. Thomas, who approached me from behind unawares. He at once addressed me with much earnestness in these·words, "Colonel, I am chagrined at the delay in your confirmation. They won't do anything I want them to do, and I begin to fear that I do you more harm than good, so I have written to Sherman and have asked him to hurry it up." I had been brevetted a brigadier-general on the 28th of March, 1864, and although a brevet at that time was a rare distinction among volunteer officers, it came too late for me. So many promotions had been made of my juniors both in rank and service, that the compliment neither pleased nor encouraged me. I was, however, grateful to Gen. Thomas for his kind and considerate interest in my behalf. It is not a slight honor to be approved by so sublime a soldier, whose figure stands out as one of the grandest the war has developed; who is conspicuous as having routed and destroyed as an organization Hood's army at Franklin and Nashville.

After the war we met again at the reunion of the Society of the Army of the Cumberland, which convened at Cincinnati. This was the first time the soldiers had met together since the restoration of peace. Many of us then met who had parted on the battle-field. Some were lying prostrate with wounds when last seen, and some appeared to us now as risen from the dead. The morning after the banquet Gen. Thomas and I were seated together in the rotunda of the Burnett House, waiting for the carriages which were to take the party to the train. The General sat apparently absorbed in thought. At length he aroused himself and said, "I can't make it out; I can't recognize these brilliant and elegant gentlemen or these eloquent orators as the same men who served under me as soldiers." Then after a pause he resumed, "But then I saw them at a disadvantage; I saw them in their blouses, unshaven and unshorn, awkward in a new role in which they had had no experience."

The General may well have been puzzled when, among the persons assembled here, such names appeared as Gen. Stanly Mathews, Manderson, Grosvenor, Jackson, Wilson, Thurston, Gross, McCook, Crufts, and many others whose names are not mentioned, not because they were less worthy, but because the list of them would be too long for the purpose in view.

The General frequently rallied me upon my large and increasing family, and said, "I think you might name one of your children for me." So when my next son was born I wrote to him announcing that "George Henry Thomas Scribner has this day reported in person for duty." The General was at that time in Washington, and by return of mail I received a document bearing all the official marks of special orders, with the following extract: "George Henry Thomas Scribner having reported in person for duty, is hereby assigned to the care of his mother until further orders."

When the boy was one year old his photograph was taken and mailed to the General's address at San Francisco, where he was then stationed. But soon after a letter with signs of mourning around it came to hand from Mrs. Thomas, informing me of the death of her husband and acknowledging the receipt of the picture. However great must have been the grief of his noble widow, the Army of the Cumberland shared it with her, and they will ever love and cherish his memory, and deplore the great loss which his comrades and his country have sustained.

On the 27th of June a desperate and disastrous assault was made upon the enemy, who were strongly entrenched, and so covered with their abattis that approach to their works was difficult and hazardous. The brigades of McCook and Mitchell, of Davis' division, and Harker's and Waggoner's brigades of Newton's division, were designated to make the charge. Every means to divert the attention of the enemy was employed. Then, all the guns that could be brought to bear upon the objective point were concentrated upon it. Then the four brigades climbed over their works and made a rush for the rebel stronghold. They had a space of some six hundred yards to cross before coming up to the main works. They also had to overcome the obstacles placed in their way. These detained them under a galling fire, and when they reached the perpendicular walls which protected the foe they found that they were unable to scale them, and as one more enterprising or fortunate succeeded in gaining the parapet, he would be instantly shot down. The attack was not successful. The ground passed over was held and fortified while the missiles of the enemy rained about them. But this scarcely compensated for the aggregate of over fifteen hundred men and officers who fell. The loss in mere numbers was to be deplored, but when I call to mind the many gallant and choice fellows that went down that day, the thought sinks like a lump of lead in my heart. It was said that Gen. Sherman wished to show Johnston that we were not afraid to fight him, and did not depend altogether upon outflanking him.

The situation was now becoming irksome. Johnston seemed disposed to hide behind his impregnable defenses. To undermine him by covered approaches was deemed too tedious and would consume too much time. These opinions gained force when it was considered that in a night Johnston could fall back to another fortified position and thereby render our labor useless. Sherman, however, determined to cut loose from his railroad and move upon Johnston's communications, and either force him to fight us upon something like equal terms or compel him to fall back to Atlanta. Once force Johnston out of this broken and easily defended country into the more open ground further south, we felt sure that we would be able to bring on a crisis where somebody would be whipped, but it wouldn't be us.

Accordingly, preparations for carrying out this plan were entered upon. McPherson was moved from the extreme left to the right. Strong works were constructed perpendicular to the rear on Sherman's left. The Third Brigade was to occupy these. My left would then be in air except that a regiment of cavalry was to hover about it. The railroad was to be abandoned. Rations for twenty days had been accumulated, and before they were consumed we expected to gain more favorable conditions. These movements were made with the utmost secrecy under cover of darkness and forests. All night of the 2d of July my men worked on the fortifications. All night long I was in my saddle directing the work; and when the morning sun revealed the formidable defenses of the enemy on the mountain it also revealed them abandoned. Johnston was again in retreat and all our labor was for naught, and Sherman had to defer his plan for marching to Johnston's rear. How Johnston always seemed to find out our intentions as soon as the critical moment arrived, I am at a loss to explain! Our movements were well screened from his view. He must have had spies among us!

No delay was made in following after the retreating columns, not even for food or rest. We hoped to overtake and bring them to a stand and force them to defend themselves before they reached other fortified positions. Passing through Marietta the Third Brigade was halted some three or four miles beyond. The next day was the glorious Fourth of July, and we made further advances to promote the cause of Liberty and Union! On the 5th and 6th we were preparing to cross the Chattahoochee, and could now discern the spires and domes of Atlanta, the objective point of the campaign, where we hoped to end these months of hardship and strife. But I was not permitted to enter with its captors. The all-night vigils of the 2d seemed to be the last feather required to break me down. A violent dysentery set in, which so exhausted my strength, that for two days I accompanied my command in an ambulance. My horse was led beside it, ready to be mounted when personal attention to the lines was deemed important. On the 6th I was unable to sit on my horse; all things seemed to swim about me, and thus I was forced to give up. The command was turned over to Col.

Given, and they carried me to the ambulance and conveyed me to the rear. I could not realize that I was so very sick, and was unreconciled and mortified at my weakness. Dr. Marks, the medical director, and Dr. Miller, my brigade surgeon, were both in kind attention upon me. I overheard Dr. Marks say, "Stimulate him, stimulate him quick, or he will slip out of your hands before you know it." This aroused me, and to show them that I was not so ill, I suddenly rose and attempted to walk, but overcome with dizziness and weakness, I pitched forward and would have fallen had they not caught me. And thus I had to yield. I became very nervous and excitable, and could not be persuaded that I was not disgraced by this surrender. To be sick was a shirk's excuse, and I felt it a great misfortune not to have been killed or wounded; and thus to be taken to the rear sick without a scratch upon my person, while so many of my comrades were disabled by honorable wounds, was felt to be a humiliation beyond endurance. Notwithstanding these hallucinations, I was at all times conscious of what was going on. They sent me to Nashville, then home, where for a time visitors were not permitted to see me. I refer thus in detail to these symptoms to show how one who was never seriously ill before was affected by this long and arduous campaign.

The beginning of the end could now be foreseen. Atlanta was doomed, and Gen. Grant's successes in the East cheered the heart of all lovers of the Union. My strength was not restored before the time of my hay-fever approach; so I determined not to be a useless expense even for the short time the government might require the services of soldiers, and I sent on my resignation, and was soon again a private citizen.

Notwithstanding the kind sympathy and generous appreciation which a grateful country has manifested toward its defenders, history records no such tangible evidence as our country has exhibited by lavish pensions to the disabled, the attractive homes for the homeless, and reverent care for the dead. Yet there are sacrifices a soldier was required to make that are rarely comprehended, and for which no adequate compensation can be made. To many, the separation from their homes was the heaviest cross they had to bear. The soldier in love with his wife, and fond of his children, had a yearning at his heart that is not taken into account when his hardships and sacrifices are computed. The soldier feels all the more, as time with its vicissitudes and bereavements overtakes him, that many happy days had been taken from his life in the prime of youth and the strength of his manhood.

The laws granting pensions to soldiers have undergone much hostile criticism from those whose lines were cast in pleasant places during the war. If these objectors would reflect a moment and try to estimate the sum of money that would induce them to stand up within range of a line of muskets and take the chances of one volley therefrom, I do not think they would consider the pittance so enormous which has been granted to many about whom bullets have rained in many battles. I have never applied for a pension myself, but I do not begrudge those who have.

CONCLUSION.

THE Third Brigade took part in the battle of Peach Tree Creek, and in that of the 22d of July, which lost us the lamented McPherson. They also had a hard fight at Jonesboro which culminated in the downfall of Atlanta. They marched with Sherman to the sea, and fought at Bentonville, their last fight of the war. The records and official papers were, of course, left at brigade headquarters, so that I am deprived of the facilities of doing justice to this fine and deserving brigade. But this has doubtless been done by my successors in command.

The Thirty-eighth suffered severely at Jonesboro, where they again distinguished themselves by charging and taking the works of the enemy and capturing many prisoners. But this brilliant achievement cost them dearly. Many brave fellows, who had passed through many hair-breadth escapes, here ended their honorable and patriotic careers. Here Capt. Osborne, of Company A, was killed. He was a corporal at Perryville. During the battle I observed him coming back from the line with blanched face and unsteady step. Upon examination of the place over which his hand was pressed, no marks of injury were found, but a hole in his haversack was discovered. A bullet had passed through its well filled contents, had penetrated his hard crackers and tin plates, and with diminished force had struck him in the pit of the stomach, which explained his sick stomach and pallid face. I assured the Corporal that he was not hurt, and sent him back to his place. But it was not long before he came back again, and, holding up a mangled hand, asked with a humble and uncertain tone, "May I go back now?"

Lieut. Low, of Company D, was at the same time shot in the head, which, like the wound of Col. Ward at New Hope Church, covered his face with blood, and made him a frightful object to behold. As Low came reeling by me, he was not so concerned for himself but that he could salute me with words of encouragement and confidence of victory. The next day when the regiment was about to start in pursuit of Bragg, Low was recognized in his place with his company. His head was covered with white bandages, whereupon he was at once ordered to the rear, but he begged to be allowed to go with us. To relieve his mind from any misgiving he might have of any unjust construction his men might put upon his going back, I peremptorily ordered him to the hospital in their presence, saying that I would not take the risk of properly taking care of him. But poor Low was hurt worse than he thought, for his skull was cracked, and it was many months before he was again fit for duty. He was captain commanding the regiment, at Bentonville, and was there killed. His commission as colonel of the regiment was on the way, but had not been received before he was called to muster in the grand army of heroic dead. Sexton, Fouts, Osborne, Peck, Southern, Dewees and Hawkins had gone before; Jenkins was soon to follow. He yet lingered, suffering agonies from a mortal wound received at Jonesboro, but the brave fellow had to die and have his name also enrolled with the Thirty-eighth's glorious detachment. At Jonesboro Griffin broke down, Carter was again wounded, Jenkins and Perry were the next in rank, but they were hopelessly wounded. Perry was shot through the lungs. The preservation of the life of this favorite officer is said to be due to the fact that the wound had become plugged with portions of his clothing, and as he lay all night upon the battle-field without attention, the chill air and prostration from the shock had so lowered his vital forces that he did not bleed to death, but after many weary months rose, as it were, from death to life.

It will be observed that the Thirty-eighth had no field officers able for duty upon their march to the sea.

Capt. Patton, who succeeded Low at Bentonville, was made colonel, Isaac Brinkworth, lieutenant-colonel, and William C. Shaw, major. These meritorious officers rose from the ranks, and passing through intermediate grades, well deserved their promotion.

And now, when about to close this record of past experiences and impressions, I pause and, glancing over what has been written, try to think what should be added to make what has been said just and proper. Like one who in preparing for a long journey leaves one trunk open until the last moment to receive any hitherto forgotten article, apprehensions disturb me and a sense of responsibility oppresses me lest injustice has been done some worthy soldier, or credit given when credit was not due, or that others should have been mentioned in connection with the events described whose names have been omitted. But I am reassured by the reflection that other books will doubtless be written from time to time, until all the facts from every point of view will be made known and justice done to all.

THE END.

INDEX.

Acton, Maj. Thomas....... 198
Allen, Lieut. M..........71, 74
Allatoona................. 237
Anderson, Camp... 125
Anderson, Gen. Robert. .20, 21
Ambrose, Capt............ 160
Atlanta Campaign.......... 237
Bald Knob................ 271
Baird, Gen. A..........140, 149
Bacon Creek............32, 35
Bardstown, Ky............ 57
Bass, Col. S. S. 32
Beatty, Gen. John.......... 85
Bingham, Lieut.-Col........ 221
Bird, Lieut. Ira 93
Bowling Green..........20, 38
Bonafon, Maj.............. 245
Bragg, Gen.......52, 54, 55, 57
  at Stone River........... 77
  pursuit of................. 185
Brinkworth, Lieut.-Col...... 311
Bridgeport................ 196
Brown's Ferry............. 118
Buel, Gen...........39, 52, 54
Buckner, Gen........20, 30, 38
Burnside, Gen. A. E........ 185
Buzzard Roost............ 223
Cameron Hill.............. 193
Carlin, Gen. W. P..169, 175, 180
Carter, Col................ 181
Chattanooga............... 170
Chapin, Col. W. R........ 67

Chickamauga, Battle of..... 139
Clapp, Dr. W. A. 36
Columbia.................. 46
Cowan.................... 46
Cox, Capt................. 73
Crittenden, Col............ 22
Crittenden, Gen. Thos. L....
  ....57, 66, 78, 84
Crufts, Gen............... 161
Culbertson, J. C........... 65
Dallas.................... 237
Davis, Gen. J. C........185, 237
Decherd................52, 53
Devol, Lieut. Geo. H.....62, 111
Devol, H. N.............65, 146
De Bruin, Capt........111, 288
Dewey, Lieut........... ... 239
Dilger, Capt...268, 271, 292, 294
Donelson.................. 39
Doyle, Barney............. 228
Elizabethtown............. 24
Ellis, Capt. E. J.........67, 72
Ely, Maj.................. 253
First Brigade, 1st Div., 14th
  Army Corps............. 112
  at Chickamauga.......... 144
  at Lookout Mountain..... 175
  at Missionary Ridge...... 178
Fitzwilliam, Lieut.......... 73
Florence.................. 44
Fouts, Capt. J. E........69, 310
Frizell, Col.........57, 67, 70

Geary, Gen............175, 176
Gilman, Capt................ 20
Gilbert, Gen................ 75
Given, Col....221, 242, 243, 305
Glover, Maj. John B......62, 70
Grant, Gen.................. 38
Gresham, Lieut.-Col. Walter
  Q........................ 62
Griffin, Lieut.-Col. D. F..62,
    67, 70, 206
  estimate of..........214, 310
Green River................ 34
Harris, Col. Len.....54, 57, 62
Hambright, Col. H. A...34,
    221, 226
Harrison, Col. Thos..... 23, 32
Hapeman, Col............. 169
Harker, Gen................ 270
Hobart, Lieut.-Col........ 221
Hollister, Lieut. Geo. H..75, 105
Hooker, Gen. Joseph........ 169
  at Lookout Mountain..171,
    172, 173, 174, 175, 177, 251
Hoover's Gap............... 122
Howard, Gen. O. O......... 168
  at Resaca...........234, 239
Humphrey, Col............. 169
Indiana, Eighty-eighth Reg. 169
  Fifty-third Reg........... 62
  Legion.................... 15
  Sixth Reg................. 22
  Twenty-Third Reg......... 17
  Tenth Battery............. 75
  Twenty-ninth Reg......... 32
  Thirtieth Reg............. 32
  Thirty-second Reg........ 34
  Thirty-seventh Reg...... 221
  Thirty-eighth Reg., 19, 26,
    32, 33, 36, 44, 46, 52, 64,
    65, 67, 69, 169

  transferred to 3d Brigade 193
  Thirty-ninth Reg......23, 32
Illinois, Twenty-fourth Reg., 221
  One Hundred and Fourth
    Reg 169
Kell, Lieut.-Col. John...67, 68
Kelso, Lieut. J. V........49, 111
Kenesaw, Battle of.....266, 300
Kentucky, Fifteenth Reg... 169
  Twenty-first Reg......... 44
Kilpatrick, Gen............ 232
King, Gen.................. 253
Lane, Gen. Jos............. 18
Low, Lieut.............309, 310
Lookout Mountain, Battle of
    171- 177
Louisville Legion.......... 22
Lytle, Gen................. 59
Maginnes, Col. E. A........ 65
Manchester................. 48
Manney, Gen............... 167
Martin, Lieut. Alex......71, 74
Maxwell, Col O. C......... 152
Mendenhall, Capt........... 85
Merriweather, Maj......22, 62
McCook, Col. Anson G..71, 145
McCook, Gen. A. McD...33
    57, 66, 78
McCook, Gen. Dan......... 160
McFeely, Gen. Robt........ 65
McPherson, Gen........... 303
McMynn, Col. 119
Miller, Col. John F......32, 84
Michigan, First Bat........ 112
  Ninth Reg................ 46
Miller, Surg. B. F.....111, 145
Miller, Gen................ 122
Mitchell, Gen.............. 43
Missionary Ridge, Battle of. 178
Miholatzy, Col............. 221

INDEX.

Morton, Gov. O. P......14, 16
  dispatch to 19, 33
Muldraugh's Hill........24, 26
Nashville.............. .38, 39
Negley, Gen. Jas. S..33, 44,
                    48, 51
Nelson, Gen............... 57
Neibling, Col...........221, 296
New Albany, Ind........11, 12
New Hope Church......... 296
Ninth Brigade........51, 57, 66
Nolinville, Tenn............ 66
Ohio, Second Reg. 64, 67, 68 71
  Forty-ninth Reg.......... 22
  Ninety-fourth Reg....57,
            67, 68, 69, 169
  Seventy-fourth Reg....... 221
  Twenty-first Reg......... 221
  Thirty-third Reg......67, 68
Orchard Knob............. 171
Osborne, Capt............. 309
Osterhaus, Gen.........171, 182
Palmer, Gen. John M. 169,
                    186, 190
Parkhurst, Col............. 46
Patton, Capt. David H...... 210
  Colonel 311
Peach Tree Creek.......... 308
Pennsylvania—Seventy-
  eighth Reg...........33, 221
  Seventy-Ninth Reg....33, 221
Perryville, Battle of.....58, 61
Price, Col................. 44
Prime, Capt............... 25
Pulaski................... 44
Redding, Joe.............. 280
Resaca, Battle of........... 232
Reynolds, Gen............. 148
Ringgold.................. 191
Rogersville................ 44

Rosecrans, Gen. W. S...63, 64
  at Stone River..77, 81, 84, 121
  at Chickamauga.......... 139
Rousseau, Gen. Lovell H.... 22
  letters to.......51, 57, 276, 278
Sanderson, Wm. L.... 17
Seventh Brigade... ....33, 43
Shepherd, Lieut.-Col........ 91
Shaw, Maj. Wm. C......... 311
Sherman, Gen. W. T. 23, 25,
       27, 28, 29, 30, 31, 32
  at Chattanooga.......170, 297
Shepherdsville, Ky......... 57
Shelbyville, Tenn.......44, 48
Sill, Gen................... 52
Sirwell, Col. Wm........53, 221
Simmonson, Capt. P.....57, 58
Spencer Grays............. 13
Springfield, Tenn.......... 64
Starkweather, Col. John.... 38
Stone River, Battle of...... 67
Stout, Col................. 242
Swaine, Capt. P. T......23, 29
Sweden's Cove....... 46
Taylor, Gen............... 13
Taylorsville, Ky............ 44
Terry, Col................. 34
Taylor's Ridge............. 191
Thomas, Gen. Geo. H...66,
                    112, 118
  after Chickamauga....... 162
  relieves Rosecrans........ 168
  anecdotes of 297, 300
Third Brigade, 1st Div., 14th
  Army Corps............. 193
Vandergrift, St. George..... 110
Van Dusen, Capt.......... 226
Van Pelt, Lieut....112, 147, 148
Van Schroeder, Col........ 108
Von Trebra, Lieut.-Col..... 34

Ward, Lieut.-Col........24, 296	Williams, Gen. A. S........ 234
Wartrace................... 48	Willich, Col................ 34
Waldron's Ridge............ 46	Wisconsin—First Reg....... 34
Wauhatchie................ 170	Tenth Reg........67, 69, 169
Whitcomb, Gov............. 13	Twenty-first Reg......... 221
Whittaker, Gen............. 232	Wood, Col. Thos. J......... 33
Willard, Capt.............. 161	Wood, Gen................ 240

www.ingramcontent.com/pod-product-compliance
Lightning Source LLC
Chambersburg PA
CBHW022021240426
43667CB00042B/1034